OUR GAME TOO

Asian Pacific Americans in Major League Baseball

By

Dr. Billy W. Simpson & Dr. Jennifer Simpson

Published by: Elevation Book Publishing
Atlanta, Georgia 30308
www.elevationbookpublishing.com

Simpson, Billy W. 1969-
Simpson, Jennifer 1979-

OUR GAME TOO:

Asian Pacific Americans in Major League Baseball p.cm.

ISBN 978-1-943904-11-2 (hc)

BISAC BIO025000
BISAC BIO016000
BISAC EDU024000
BISAC HIS030000
BISAC JNF054010
BISAC SPO003030

Contents

Dedication.. 7

Acknowledgments... 8

Special Acknowledgment... 13

Chapter One.. 14

Introduction... 14

The Reason... 14

Baseball and Diversity 15

Summary 18

Chapter Two.. 22

Baseball in Asia 22

Introduction... 22

Part I: History.. 22

China 23

Japan 24

Taiwan 27

Korea 28

Philippines... 29

Other Asian Nations 30

Part II: Performance.. 31

Little League.. 31

The Olympics 32

World Baseball Classic...................................... 33

Asian Games.. 33

Summary.. 34

Chapter Three 35

The Curious Case of Honolulu Johnny and the Prince 35

Introduction..35

Honolulu Johnny...35

The Prince..40

Summary..44

Chapter Four...46

Bobby Balcena: The Asian-American Jackie Robinson......46

Summary..50

Chapter Five 51

The 1960s 51

Introduction..51

Masanori Murakami 52

Tony Solaita 55

Summary..62

Chapter Six 64

The 1970s 64

Introduction..64

Wendell Kim 65

Lenn Sakata..67

Ryan Kurosaki 73

Summary 74

Batting Statistics for the 1970s 75

Chapter Seven 76

The 1980s..76

Introduction..76

Atlee Hammaker 77

Summary 88

Chapter Eight..90

The 1990s 90

Introduction 90

Benny Agbayani 90

Danny Graves 93

Johnny Damon 97

Wilbur Wakamatsu 106

Onan Masaoka 107

Summary 108

The 2000s 110

Introduction 110

Kurt Suzuki 111

Travis Ishikawa 113

Brandon League 114

Billy Sadler 115

Shane Komine 115

Charlie Zink 116

Dane and Bronson Sardinha 117

Shane Victorino 121

Jeremy Guthrie 123

Clay Rapada 124

Geno Espineli 130

Tim Lincecum 130

Chris Aguila 132

Wes Littleton 132

Matt Tuiasosopo 133

Brandon Villafuerte 133

Jason Bartlett 133

Summary 134

Chapter Ten 137

    The 2010s 137

    Introduction 137

    Hank Conger 138

    Rob Refsnyder 139

    Sean Manaea 142

    Tommy Pham 142

    Darwin Barney 143

    Kolten Wong 144

    Addison Russell 145

    Summary 147

Chapter Eleven 149

    The Future of Asian Pacific American Baseball 149

    Introduction 149

    Diversity in the MLB 149

    Diversity Initiatives 151

    Hall of Fame 154

    Future 154

Appendices 156

Endnotes 162

References 178

Dedication

This book is dedicated to our son, Jack. We love you more than anything. As you grow up, remember that life only gives you so many fastballs down the middle, so swing! The game and life are both too short to keep the bat on your shoulder.

Mom and Dad

Acknowledgments

Dr. Billy W. Simpson:

For as long as I can remember, I have loved baseball. I love everything about the game: the smells, the history, the sounds, everything. There's not too much that compares with the feeling of standing in the batter's box and connecting solidly with a pitch, the echo from the "crack" of a wood bat that comes only from the purest of hits, and watching your line drive find a home, untouched, in the green grass of the outfield; the dirt flying up from your cleats as you round third base hard on your way home, watching the catcher's eyes and your teammate's motions to see if you need to "get down;" or the feeling of satisfaction of helping your team that comes from a batting-glove high-five when you cross the plate. From playing baseball as a young kid, playing in competitive adult wood-bat baseball leagues, and playing in various Major League Baseball Fantasy Camps as a "grown-up" kid in my 30s and 40s, this game means more to me than I can say. Actually, as we were completing this book in 2017, I have decided that this summer will be the end of my baseball-playing career. It will end on Memorial Day weekend, when I will be privileged to play a game at Fenway Park in Boston, my final game ever; something that my 12-year-old self, throwing a ball against the bricked side of Pine Knot Elementary School next door to where my Grandma lived, could have never even dared to dream. What a perfect place for *this* part of my baseball life to end. But it's not the end of my love affair with this game. My little boy, Jack, is nine years old and his baseball career is just starting. He's already a better player than I ever was. I am so proud of his heart, determination, and love for baseball. This seems wonderfully familiar. Like his dad, he loves baseball; it's something that we have always shared. From taking Jack to various baseball camps, to coaching his regular season and his all-star teams, I love being a "baseball dad" more than I ever loved being a baseball player. People sometimes shake their head in bewilderment and ask me why I love baseball so much and why I have continued to play this game into my 40s, spending lots of money, lots of time, and traveling all over the eastern United States *just* to play baseball. If I really were to be honest, really honest, and tell them, or you, the true and unfiltered reasons why I have continued to play the game, and why I have continued to chase whatever baseball dream it is I've been chasing, you would cry. So let me just say that for me baseball is about redemption, and that those of us who have went without, are often the most driven to make things as they should have always been. Our time on this planet, and on the diamond, is way too brief.

My favorite baseball player is not profiled in this book, yet he is on every page, woven into every word I have written, and into every minute I have spent researching. He is the reason not only for this book, but he is my reason for living. So I would like to thank my son, Jack, for being the answer to every prayer that I have prayed. My love for you, son, is unchangeable, unbreakable, and it knows no end. If I am remembered in life for one thing, I hope it is simply for being your dad. I am so proud of you, not because of your baseball ability or anything else, but just because you are you, and you are mine. I love you.

I would like to thank my wife, Jennifer. You have stood with me in times of joy and sorrow. You know me like no one else does, and still, you love me. Thank you for letting me continue to play baseball for so long and for understanding why. Thank you for everything you do for our family and for the example you set for our little boy. While the idea of this book was mine, the determination to make it a reality was yours. You are beautiful, inside and out. Thank you for writing this book with me; I am so glad we get to share this together. When it comes to "baseball wives" and "baseball moms," Jack and I know that you are the MVP.

I would like to thank my parents, Wayne and Georgia Simpson, for showing me that love is about sacrifice and family above anything else. Although you may not have ever really loved baseball, you loved me, and I have always known that. I love you so much, Mom and Dad. Thank you also to Jennifer's parents for accepting me as your son, and for raising an amazing daughter; I love you Jim Cox, and Jim and Jackie Brown. Jack is blessed to have the best grandparents ever!

Thank you to the rest of my family, the Simpsons, and the Creekmores. Thank you to my Grandparents, who though they are not still with us, live in my heart every day. I tell Jack stories of Arnold and Etta Simpson, and of Clellan and Mary Creekmore often. Thank you to two uncles who helped inspire the love of baseball in me as a child, Ed Hill and Dorman Spradlin, your stories of baseball long ago and your love for the game will never be forgotten.

Thank you to the friends that I have made through playing baseball as a kid, and as an adult in the East Tennessee Adult Baseball League, the Pine Mountain Men's Baseball League, the Bernie Carbo Baseball Fantasy Camp, the Boston All-Star Baseball Fantasy Camp, the Official Boston Red Sox Baseball Fantasy Camp, and the Columbus Baseball Legends Reds/Indians Fantasy Camp. It has been a privilege to be your friend and teammate. Baseball truly is a brotherhood. Thank you to the Boston Red Sox and the Cincinnati Reds, the teams that have held my baseball heart since I was a kid. Thank you to the National Baseball Hall of Fame, and the Cincinnati Reds Hall of Fame and Museum, the finest baseball museum outside of Cooperstown. Thank you to Bernie Carbo, Tom Kennedy, Mike Talis, Larry Marino, and Hung Tran for providing outstanding and competitive baseball camps for me to play at over the years with wonderful MLB legends. Thanks also to my friends from my hometown of Pine Knot and McCreary County, Kentucky; for being part of our life and for letting me, Jennifer, and Jack be part of yours. There's nowhere that we would rather call home.

Thank you to McCreary County Public Schools and the University of the Cumberlands, two great educational organizations who put the interests of their communities and students first. It is an honor for Jennifer, Jack, and me to be part of such wonderful and distinguished institutions. We are grateful.

Thank you to our church, Christ the King Anglican Mission of Pine Knot, KY. for being a haven of hope, and thanks be to God for his mercy and love. Thank you to the men and women of the United States military, our law enforcement, and first responders who put their lives on the line every day for what we hold so dear in this wonderful country.

Thank you to the men and women who fought for equality in baseball and the nation. For the courage to take the field in the face of adversity and intolerance, for the courage to be who you are, and for making baseball a game for everyone. It is a true honor, in some small way, to tell some of your stories. Finally, enjoy the book; it has been written in conditions and places that you would not believe. I hope it touches your heart, I hope it informs you, and I hope it makes you love baseball just a little more.

"Our Game Too"

Dr. Jennifer Simpson:

First and foremost, I thank the Lord for all the blessings you have given me. Next, I would like to thank Bill for being the best teammate in life. I love you. Thank you to Jack for being the inspiration to be the best person I can every day. I cannot wait to see how you will make the world a better place. I would also like to thank our family: The Coxes, Harmons, Browns, Simpsons, and Creekmores. Specifically, thanks to my parents, Jim and Jackie, for encouraging me to love learning. You were my first teachers. Also, thank you to my second parents (my in-laws), Wayne and Georgia, for all that you do for our family.

For some, this may not seem like a project you would see with my name on the cover of, but it combines two things I have always enjoyed. I remember the moment I fell in love with reading non-fiction through a borrowed library book, the biography of Paul Revere. Since then, and many biographies and autobiographies later, I still enjoy reading this genre. As far as the content, for as long as I can remember I have followed the Cincinnati Reds. Bill and I had the pleasure of taking my dad and sister to their first games, and I look forward to taking my niece to see the Reds next. There is no other sport that compares to baseball. The combination of biographical research and baseball has made this project enjoyable, and not "work." I have truly enjoyed working with Bill to create profiles on these MLB players and coaches.

A special thanks to my colleagues and friends in the Department of Leadership Studies for their encouragement: Drs. Vann, Coleman, and Hollingsworth, and Mrs. Debbie Wood. I would also like to thank the University of the Cumberlands. I am honored to work at an institution that I love.

Special Acknowledgment

Bill and Jennifer would like to say a special thanks to our friend Bryan Kuhn, who has supplied many of the photos for this book from his extensive historical baseball collection, and took the lead in coordinating and chasing down all of the other photos within these pages. Bryan went from being "some dude I met at baseball camp" years ago to being a wonderful and true family friend. From day one at baseball camp, he made me feel like I belonged. He is a baseball historian and lover of the game. Thank you so much for your contributions to this book.

Chapter One

Introduction

The Reason

It was a warm summer evening, under an April sky in rural southeastern Kentucky, at a Little League Baseball field when my seven year old son, Jack, stepped up to the plate. This was his first at-bat in organized Little League Baseball. The first pitch that Jack saw passed him for a strike, but on the next pitch he lined a single into centerfield. His mom cheered for Jack to run, and my little guy hustled down to first base with his arms stretched out behind him like a superhero flying through a sky of dirt and clay. In many ways, he was a superhero, to me at least. Tears welled up in my eyes for reasons that I still cannot quite explain. I was so proud that on that seemingly uneventful day in small-town Kentucky USA, two of my greatest loves, my son and baseball, had found each other. The tears were there for other reasons, too. They were partially due to the joy that even in 2014, *this* was actually happening, and partially due to the realization that my little boy was growing up, and that no matter what might follow, I would never be able to fully shelter him from the harshness of this world. At this point, you might be wondering why this was such a big deal; surely on this day, there were thousands of other dads on thousands of other baseball fields in thousands of other towns across the country feeling this same flood of emotion. It is a big deal because my son Jack is Asian-American, and our town doesn't have a great deal of diversity. Our county is located right in the middle of a naturally beautiful area of Appalachia that is suffering from poverty and related problems, due to the decline of the coal mining industry and other factors. It is important to understand that the poverty line is not a measurement of morality or common decency, and most of the people in our area are thoughtful and genuinely good. People from outside this area might assume that intolerance and ignorance are a way of life in Appalachia and rural America; that however, is a lazy and archaic stereotype that could not be farther from the truth. Of course there are both good and bad people here, just as there are in *every* part of this country.

The fact that our local Little League Baseball and our area is starting to grow in diversity brings pride and happiness to my heart; and hope for all that lies ahead. Our family is accepted and loved in this town, and it is a place that we are proud to call home. Jack has wonderful teammates and friends who love him and love us. I believe that positive change is steadily happening in small-town USA. For our town, in our time, and on a smaller scale, Jack is not a lot different than Jackie Robinson or any other athlete or person who has been brave enough to break a barrier, leading others to embrace our differences as strengths.

Baseball and Diversity

For as long as baseball has been baseball, it has been a game that has been slow to accept change. That remains the case today, even though players are welcomed into professional baseball from all backgrounds and from all parts of the world, recent statistics show that the an unofficial "color line" of sorts still exists beyond the field, into virtually all levels of coaching, management, and administration. In 2015, when the Seattle Mariners fired manager Lloyd McClendon, it marked the first time since 1987 that there had been no African-American managers in Major League Baseball. This lasted until early 2016 when the Dodgers hired former MLB outfielder Dave Roberts, who is also Asian Pacific-American, as their manager. As recent as 2009, the number of minority managers and coaches in MLB was much more in line with the percentage of minority players in the big leagues. This situation has not gone unrecognized by Major League Baseball, and to its credit, the league has attempted to enact policies and procedures to fix the problem. In 1999, former MLB Commissioner Bud Selig sent a memo to all owners and general managers directing them to consider minority candidates for all managerial, general manager, and scouting administrative positions. The "Selig Rule," as it came to be known, seemed to have a positive effect in the short-term. However, by 2016, the same inequality has reemerged. When Rob Manfred replaced Selig as MLB Commissioner in 2015, he once again issued a similar directive. Today, the number of African-Americans playing Major League Baseball is just under ten percent, a number that finally seems to be at least holding steady after years of decline, despite numerous efforts to make the game more accessible to inner-city kids, and kids all over the United States, through MLB-funded programs like the RBI initiative.

We are now over sixty years removed from April 15, 1947, when Jackie Robinson broke the "color barrier" by becoming the first African-American player in MLB's modern era as an infielder for the Brooklyn Dodgers. Although a color barrier never officially existed as a written rule or official policy, it was a definitive social expectation for baseball, which some have ironically called a "gentlemen's agreement," an agreement that owners were very reluctant to buck against or openly question. While there were two black players before Robinson who had played in the major leagues, William White who appeared in one game in 1879, and Moses Walker who played a full major league season in 1884, there was a sixty-three year period of shameful baseball segregation prior to Jackie Robinson. The struggles and heroic efforts of Robinson are well documented in print and film and constituted a significant turning point toward making "America's pastime" truly accessible for *all* Americans. The period immediately following Robinson's historic feat and extending through 1984 had shown an increase in black players in MLB, hitting a high of 18.7% in 1981. The percentage of black players then started to decline, as the percentage of white players started to increase for the first time since Robinson's entrance in MLB in 1947. The effect of Robinson reverberated throughout equality movements in American society. United States civil rights pioneer Martin Luther King Jr. once told Dodgers star Don Newcombe, another former Negro Leaguer, "You'll never know what you and Jackie and Roy [Campanella] did to make it possible for me to do my job."

While Robinson helped pave the way for all minority baseball players, the color barriers that existed for players of Latino and Asian backgrounds followed a very different timeline. Before 1947, MLB teams looking for talent would sometimes turn to Latino or Native American players who were light-skinned enough to be deemed "acceptable" by the baseball establishment, or at least acceptable enough to be overlooked as violators of the color barrier. While some light-skinned Latino players were permitted to play in MLB, the darker skinned players were forced to play in the Negro Leagues. There are many stories of African-American players who baseball teams tried to list them as Puerto Rican, Cuban, or Native American in an effort to get them into the league. This is not to say that Latino baseball players were actually welcome in baseball in the era prior to Robinson; they also faced despicable acts of discrimination and prejudice.

Summary

The contribution of Asian Pacific-Americans, which in this book includes Americans who identify as being of Asian heritage and/or Pacific Islander heritage, in professional baseball is an increasingly relevant topic in our society. The history of this group in baseball has been largely overlooked and significantly undervalued. Previous works on specific individuals or baseball in internment camps have been documented, but a holistic examination of Asian Pacific-American baseball player profiles is missing from the current printed format and websites.

The story of America's Pastime is filled with profiles and tales of early players who pioneered change and equality in the game of baseball. In recent decades, the influx of Asian and Asian Pacific-Americans in professional baseball here in the United States has been significant, but the groundwork for inclusion and acceptance was laid by players as early as the turn of the twentieth century through struggle and perseverance. While the heroic story of baseball legend Jackie Robinson breaking the "color barrier" of baseball in 1947 is well-known and documented by numerous books and the recent critically-acclaimed motion picture "42," the story of the struggle for inclusion by Asian and Asian Pacific-American baseball players is quite unique, with its own pioneers and heroes who have virtually gone unnoticed, unrecognized, and their stories untold. Much has been written about the important role of African-Americans in breaking down barriers and stereotypes, but little has been written about similar struggles and triumphs by Asian Pacific-American baseball players in the United States.

This is a rich history full of fascinating and heroic individuals with stories waiting to be told.

This book is targeted toward the millions of baseball fans in the United States and around the world who will hopefully be captivated by what has, until now, been a somewhat "invisible" part of baseball literature. The following chapters provide an entertaining and thought-provoking look into the history of Asian Pacific-Americans in Major League baseball through anecdotes, stories, and narrative timelines. Many Asian Pacific-American baseball pioneers are profiled and finally given their rightful place in Major League baseball history and lore. The Asian Pacific-Americans profiled in each chapter are included in the decade in which they debuted in major league baseball, although their careers often span multiple decades.

While many Americans have traditionally considered baseball to be our national pastime, several Asian countries consider baseball in the same vein. The second chapter of this book explores baseball internationally, focusing on the sport in several Asian and Pacific nations. International success of Asian baseball programs is also examined.

"Our Game Too"

Bobby Balcena

(Courtesy of the Cincinnati Reds)

After an overview of baseball's importance in Asian culture, the curious case of Honolulu Johnny and other early Hawaiian baseball pioneers are presented. Then Bobby Balcena is profiled as an important Asian Pacific-American baseball player who is sometimes referred to as the "Asian-American Jackie Robinson." The focus of the book then shifts to Masanori Murakami and the influx of Asians and Asian Pacific-Americans into baseball in the 1960s. The following chapters look at the evolution of baseball for Asian Pacific American players from the 1970s to the 2016 season. Finally, an analysis of the future of baseball for Asian Pacific-American players is offered. There are over forty MLB players and coaches profiled in the upcoming narrative. While every effort has been made to include all Asian Pacific-American MLB players, some may have been inadvertently and unintentionally left out. The inclusion of players in this book was based on published articles, books, and media interviews available at the time of printing.

Chapter Two

Baseball in Asia

Introduction

The impact and presence of Asian Pacific-Americans in baseball today would not be possible without the introduction of baseball to Asian culture. Through war, religion, and education reforms, baseball was brought to Asian soil. The game was spread to many Asian countries at a time when it was truly a way of life for Americans, and as Americans traveled the globe for a multitude of reasons, baseball went with them. This chapter focuses on the history of baseball in Asian nations, and explores how Asian nations perform internationally in baseball today.

Part I: History

Baseball, an American invention and undoubtedly the national pastime, was once seen as a tool for western missionaries to spread Christianity throughout the world. Although the history of how the game was developed is controversial, scholars generally agree that in the 1800s, baseball began to take root in American soil. Abner Doubleday was credited with creating baseball in 1839 in the United States, and Alexander Cartwright developed the rules in 1845. It was several years, however, before baseball reached Asia. American missionaries, soldiers, and educators are credited with spreading the sport to most Asian nations. Baseball reached Shanghai, China in 1863 and was later introduced in Japan, Korea, Taiwan, Mongolia, India, and the Philippines.

"Our Game Too"

China

Although baseball was first introduced in China in the 1860s by Christian missionaries, the sport has not become as popular in China as it has in other Asian nations. Baseball was banned during the Cultural Revolution (formerly known as the Great Proletarian Cultural Revolution) in China during the 1960s by Mao Zedong[i], and it did not reemerge until after his death in 1976. The ban was based on baseball's western roots;[ii] however, baseball can be closely linked to Confucian ideas. Confucianism ideas align with baseball through the absence of a time clock, and through individuals sacrificing themselves for the betterment of the team. The history of baseball in China is intertwined with youthful fascination and the establishment's fear of Americanization.

In the 1870s, groups of male students were sent from China to the United States as part of the Chinese Educational Mission. The intent was for the students to learn more advanced Western fields, and then to return to China after fifteen years to serve the Chinese government. In addition to their formal education, the students formed an organized baseball squad in 1876 in Hartford called the "Oriental Base-Ball Club[iii]". The Chinese Educational Mission program was cut short in 1881, however, by the Chinese government. The young men were required to return home after reports surfaced that the students had become too Americanized, as partially evidenced by their love and participation in baseball.

With the establishment of the first Young Men's Christian Association (YMCA) in Tianjin, China in 1895, physical exercise became more accepted in Chinese culture. In 1905, the first mainland baseball game between two Chinese teams took place in Shanghai. War with Japan, followed by a civil war impacted the game in China. In areas where American troops had bases, baseball equipment availability helped to popularize the sport. During the Cultural Revolution in the 1960s, however, baseball was non-existent in mainstream China. In the 1980s and 1990s, the Chinese government promoted baseball as a tool to gain status from other nations. China related most closely to the Japanese version of baseball, as opposed to connecting their developing sport to the American style.

The China Baseball League was formed in 2002, but it trails behind basketball in popularity in China.[iv] Limited Chinese government funding lead to the MLB introducing baseball to elementary schools, providing funding, and increasing media presence in recent years. The highlight of baseball in China in recent years was China's defeat of Taiwan during the 2008 Beijing Olympics.

Japan

In the same era, many changes were taking place in Japan after the fall of Tokugawa Bakufu, a feudal Japanese government led by shoguns from 1603 to 1967. The trend included more westernization in learning and leisure. Baseball was introduced to Japan in 1872 by American professor Horace Wilson[v]. Wilson was a former civil war soldier, as well as a history and English teacher. He was brought to Japan to help modernize the Japanese educational system. While teaching in Japan, he determined that his students needed more physical activity to expand their curriculum. He taught his students the game of baseball, and it quickly caught on. Albert Bates, another teacher from America, organized the first seven-inning game for the students against their foreign instructors.[vi] The popularity of baseball in Japan grew steadily. By 1878, Shimbasi Athletic Club, founded by Shiki Masaoka, became the first baseball club. This was the first organized baseball team in Japan.

While the rules of baseball may be generally uniform worldwide, culturally there are additional tenets that are accepted throughout the Asian nations that impact the game. These commandments are known in Japan as the "Samurai Code of Conduct for Baseball Players." They include:

The player must be a total team member.

The player must follow an established procedure.

The player must undergo hard training.

The player must play for the team.

The player must demonstrate fighting spirit.

The player must behave like a gentleman on the field.

The player must not be materialistic.

The player must be careful in comments to the press.

The player must follow the rule of sameness.

The player must behave like a good Japanese person off the field.

The player must recognize and respect the team "pecking" order.

The player must strive for team harmony and unity. [vii]

Additionally, one enjoying a game in Japan may notice a subtle difference on the scoreboard, an additional column labeled "B." The B is for base on balls, or walks; while it does not directly impact the score, even a walk is given greater importance through their view of putting the team first. This supports the notion that, in many ways, Japan has made baseball *their* own sport.

Through their attempts at colonization in Taiwan and Korea, Japan spread baseball to other Asian nations. Although originally imitating the United States, the Japanese influence on baseball was attractive to nations who shared similar cultural values. Discipline, diligence, and determination (as evidenced by the Samurai Code above) are key factors to the success of baseball in Asian countries.

The birth of professional Japanese baseball is linked to the "Father of Japanese American Baseball," Kenichi Zenimura. Also known as the "Dean of the Diamond," Zenimura was born in Japan but moved to Hawaii at the age of fifteen. Zenimura brought goodwill baseball tours between 1922 and 1937 to Japan, Korea, and Manchuria.[viii] The 1934 tour of Japan by U.S. Major League Baseball players, most notably Babe Ruth, demonstrated the Japanese fans' emerging love and infatuation with baseball. The recruiting of players around Japan to compete against the United States All-Stars lead to what would become the Japan Tokyo baseball club.[ix]

In 1936, the Japanese Professional League, modeled after the American major leagues, was founded. The outbreak of World War II lead to anti-American and anti-baseball sentiment in Japan. At one point, baseball was even banned in that country. Baseball, however, survived in Japan. In fact, due to baseball's popularity in Japan, the United States military considered sending Babe Ruth to Guam to create radio broadcasts in Japan requesting their surrender. During the American occupation following Japan's surrender, American General Douglas MacArthur prioritized reopening baseball stadiums as opposed to sumo stables. This helped re-establish and propel baseball as Japan rebounded from effects of World War II.

While players from Japan would begin coming to the United States to play Major League Baseball in the 1960s, the first Japanese-American major league baseball player was pitcher Ryan Kurosaki, who debuted for the St. Louis Cardinals in 1975 and is profiled later in the book.[x]

Taiwan

Baseball is currently the most popular sport in Taiwan, but there has been a tumultuous and scandalous history for the game in the small nation. While under Japanese rule in 1895, baseball was introduced in Taiwan. Most Taiwanese consider 1968 as the official start of baseball there, as the popularity soared with the defeat of the Japanese defending Little League World Champions by the Red Leaf Little Leaguers.[xi]

The following year, Taiwan entered the worldwide Little League, and with much success. Taiwan has won the Little League World Series a record seventeen times between 1969 and 2016. Their quick rise to success lead to multiple investigations of Taiwan teams. However, all findings indicated that Taiwan Little League teams played within the Little League Baseball rules and guidelines.

The Chinese Professional Baseball League (Taiwan) was formed in 1990, with a total of four teams owned by major corporations. The league was not without its share of scandal, though. In 1997, some professional Taiwanese players admitted to fixing games as part of a gambling scandal. Additionally in 1997, members of Taiwan's Pintung High School baseball championship team were threatened by gangsters betting on the high school championship. Today, the Chinese Professional Baseball League in Taiwan is considered the second best professional league in Asia, behind the professional baseball leagues of Japan.

Korea

In the same time period, Korea was facing an increase in the importance of physical exercise, similar to Japan. In 1905, American missionary Philip Gillett introduced baseball in Korea. [xii]   Gillett was the general secretary of the YMCA's International Committee for Korea. [xiii]   Japanese soldiers occupying Korea from 1905 to 1945 further propelled the popularity of baseball.   Many Koreans perceived baseball to be an export of Japan, and through playing, their occupiers gave the Koreans an opportunity to defeat their oppressors. It became a symbol of pride. Baseball was limited to virtual non-existence during World War II, as well as during the Korean War.

As part of the United Nations agreement following World War II, Korea was divided at the 38th parallel. The Soviet Union occupied the northern portion, while the United States occupied the southern portion. This division led to the formation of two separate Koreas. The Democratic People's Republic of Korea (communist) is more commonly referred to as North Korea, while the Republic of Korea (democratic) is known as South Korea. The presence of American troops in South Korea helped to maintain an interest in the sport during these difficult times. Both North and South Korea are currently members of the International Baseball federation. Since their official division, South Korea has developed and excelled as an economic and technological power, while North Korea has struggled. South Korea has also experienced significant success in baseball.

Political and social tensions prompted the formation of the Korean Baseball Organization to unite the nation of South Korea in 1981. The inaugural season began in March of 1982 with six teams. Rules for players in the league included no drinking alcohol, no smoking, no playing cards, abstinence, and clean hygiene. The intense training for players included fielding grounders and line drives from fifteen to thirty feet from the fielders. Although the league is quite popular in Korea, many of the best Korean players play in Japan for economic reasons, and in recent years, have started playing in the United States.

Violence and political agendas have affected baseball in Korea more than any other nation in Asia. While American and Japanese influences introduced and fostered baseball in Korea, their adaptation of the support is uniquely Korean. One of the recent highlights that cemented Korea's place internationally in baseball occurred during the 2000 Olympics, with a bronze medal win. To many, a third place finish in the world showcase may not seem like a highlight. To Korea, however, the defeat of Japan for the medal was Asian baseball at its best and resulted in celebrations across the nation.

Philippines

Late in the 19th century, American soldiers introduced baseball to the Philippines. The first league and teams formed in the Philippines were comprised of the soldiers, but interest in baseball soon spread to the Filipinos. Baseball quickly grew in popularity in the Philippines and spread to rural areas, where children played the sport in loincloths. The popularity of baseball steadily diminished, though, as United States troops withdrew from the Philippines after World War II. The lack of equipment donated by troops and coaching were contributing factors that lead to a decline in baseball's popularity. Basketball has since replaced baseball as a prominent sport in the Philippines. [xiv]

Other Asian Nations

Through war, occupation, religious missions, and education, baseball has spread to other Asian nations as well. Many national teams in Asia participate in the Asian Baseball Championship, founded by the Baseball Federation of Asia in 1954. Since 1983, the Asian Baseball Championship has also served as the Olympic baseball qualifying tournament for the region[xv].

Mongolia

The Mongolian Baseball National Federation was organized in 1991. The National team has struggled greatly in international competition. In February 2017, the Mongolian Olympic Committee announced an initiative to increase support of the country's baseball program in preparation for the 2020 Summer Olympics in Tokyo. In 2017, the baseball team was ranked 56th in the World Baseball and Softball Confederation rankings.[xvi]

Thailand

Baseball was officially established in Thailand in 1992 with the formation of the Amateur Baseball Association of Thailand. Efforts to increase youth baseball development began in Thailand in 2001. There are three primary amateur leagues in the country: Little League, minor league, and major league. The national team competes in many international competitions, including the Asian Cup.[xvii]

"Our Game Too"

Pakistan

The governing body of baseball in Pakistan is the Pakistan Baseball federation, founded in 1992. This was around the same time that the sport was introduced to the nation. The national team qualified for the World Baseball Classic qualifier round for the first time in 2016.

Hong Kong

Baseball was originally introduced in Hong Kong during World War II by American soldiers. Little league was formally introduced in Hong Kong in 1972. The Hong Kong Baseball Association was later formed in 1993 to develop the game in youth leagues, schools, universities, and in international competitions. The Baseball Asia website reports that the number of people playing baseball in Hong Kong has increased since these efforts began. [xviii]

Part II: Performance

As baseball spread across Asia, several nations have excelled internationally. Through Little League International, the World Baseball Classic, the Olympics, and the Asian games, the popularity and development of baseball in Asia is consistent and, in many cases, growing. As more youth are involved in Little League and Asian nations experience success, the future of baseball in the region is promising to say the least.

Little League

The Little League World Series, originally known as the National Little League Tournament, was first played in 1947[xix]. American teams dominated the championship until 1957, when

Industrial- Monterrey (Mexico) became the first international team to take the honors. Ten years later, a team from Japan won their first Little League World Series championship in 1967. Teams from Japan have won the championship ten times through 2015. Taiwan has dominated the series, as far as Asian teams are concerned, with a total of seventeen championships. South Korea is the only other Asian nation to win the title, with a total of three championships. Interestingly, of the past five years, four Asian teams have won the series (Japan with three titles, and South Korea with one). This domination of baseball in the Little League organization demonstrates the level of commitment that the youth, volunteers, and parents place on baseball in many these Asian nations.

The Olympics

Baseball became an official Olympic sport in 1992 but was eliminated in the 2012 games. In the few short years of Olympic baseball, Japan earned three medals, South Korea earned two medals, and Taiwan earned one medal. South Korea won gold at the 2008 Olympics in Beijing, China.[xx] Since the departure of baseball from the Olympics, the World Baseball Federation still ranks Japan, Taiwan, and South Korea in the top ten teams in the world. In early 2016, it was announced that the Tokyo Olympic Organizing Committee would recommend that baseball be restored to the summer Olympics in 2020 when the event will be held in Tokyo. The decision to restore baseball was officially announced in August 2016.[xxi] Many Asian countries are already preparing in an attempt to qualify and compete in the event.

"Our Game Too"

World Baseball Classic

After baseball was eliminated from the Olympics, a FIFA (soccer) World Cup style baseball tournament was created. The World Baseball Classic was founded in 2005, and deems the winner the "World Champion." [xxii] Professional players from leagues around the world are encouraged to participate with their national team. The tournament has been played four times, including the 2017 WBC. Japan won two World Baseball Classic titles (2006, 2009) and placed third in 2013. South Korea placed second in 2009, and third in 2006. The United States has not won the World Baseball Classic as of 2016, perhaps due to many of the United States best players not playing in the games because of possibility of injury or missing part of MLB Spring Training, either of which could affect their career in professional baseball.

Six teams from Asia participated in the 2017 World Baseball Classic. Japan, China, South Korea, and Chinese Taipei were all selected for the 2017 World Baseball Classic, while the Philippines was admitted to the tournament as a Qualifier team. The tournament began March 6, 2017 at locations around the world. [xxiii]

Asian Games

Next to the Olympics, the Asian Games are the most prestigious of competitions in Asia. Currently there are competitions in eighty-eight different sports. [xxiv] Only a few Asian countries have dominated baseball in the Asian Games. Baseball was added to the Asian Games in 1994 with a total of six teams competing that first year. The countries participating included China, Japan, South Korea, Taiwan, Mongolia, and Thailand. In 1998 through 2006, the Philippines participated, while Mongolia did not. In 2010 and 2014, the field expanded to eight teams with participation from Japan, South Korea, Taiwan, China, Pakistan, Mongolia, Hong Kong, and Thailand. South Korea, Taiwan (Chinese Taipei), and Japan have each earned six medals in the games, which are held every four years (See Table Below). China has placed fourth in all six competitions.

Year	Gold	Silver	Bronze
1994	Japan	South Korea	Taiwan
1998	South Korea	Japan	Taiwan
2002	South Korea	Taiwan	Japan
2006	Taiwan	Japan	South Korea
2010	South Korea	Taiwan	Japan
2014	South Korea	Taiwan	Japan

Summary

In forty years, baseball went from a new game to a professional spectator sport, and finally to America's national pastime. Around the same time, Asian immigrants and Asian Pacific-Americans began developing their own teams in the United States. In 1899, Takie Okumura founded the Excelsiors in Hawaii.[xxv] In 1903, Chiura Obata founded the first Japanese American baseball team in San Francisco. It was known as the Fuji Athletic club. Wherever Asian communities developed on American soil, baseball became part of their daily life. It was the beginning of an American love affair with baseball that, at its roots, was not bound by color or ethnicity.

Chapter Three

The Curious Case of Honolulu Johnny and the Prince

Introduction

It seems fitting that the first Asian and Asian Pacific-American players to appear in Major League Baseball games came from the Hawaiian Islands, an American state that links the continental United States to the Asian continent geographically, economically, and culturally. Today, Hawaii is the only state in the USA with a "minority majority" with over fifty percent of the state claiming Asian Pacific Islander heritage.[xxvi] The game of baseball started to thrive in the late nineteenth century Hawaii on sugar plantations and related industries. The early development of the game there is quite similar to its development in the Caribbean, which was also home to many sugar plantations.

Honolulu Johnny

John Brodie Williams was born in 1889 in the, then, Kingdom of Hawaii,[xxvii] some seventy-nine years before it would become an American state, although only nine years before Hawaii became a United States' territory. The Hawaiian monarchy was overthrown in 1893, and the nation existed as the Republic of Hawaii until it was annexed by the United States in 1898. Under the United States Organic Act of 1900, native Hawaiians, even those who had been born in the Kingdom of Hawaii, such as John Williams, were conferred United States citizenship.[xxviii]

The Kingdom of Hawaii had seen a large influx of Asian immigrants for many years, which had helped to create and redefine a distinctly Hawaiian culture. While the islands were originally settled by Polynesians, the eighteenth and nineteenth century brought many Asian immigrants to Hawaii via its location as an important trade center between the United States and Asian countries.[xxix] Later the immigrants began to work on sugar plantations. Many native-born Hawaiians are descended from those immigrants. This Asian Pacific Islander culture has been significant in the history of Hawaii.

John Williams was the son of a British immigrant who moved to the United States as an infant and was raised mostly in the Cleveland, Ohio area. Williams' mother was born in Hawaii to a Hawaiian mother and white father. His father and mother met in Hawaii when his father was working as a photographer in the islands. When Williams was growing up in Hawaii, the plantations had many different baseball teams, and playing the game was the primary source of recreation for both men and boys. Johnny had several brothers and sisters, many of whom played baseball to some degree and were well-known players in Hawaii in the early 1900s. One newspaper also noted that Williams' father had played for a baseball club near Cleveland, although this is somewhat unsubstantiated.[xxx]

Williams' baseball career in Hawaii began at an early age on the baseball fields of Honolulu, and he started to gain notice as a very good player while in grade school. He also went on to play in adult baseball leagues in Hawaii. Williams was a noted pitcher who also seemed to have some ability as a hitter. When Johnny represented his Hawaiian club team against a visiting mainland American team of semi-pro players in 1910, pitching a no-hitter in one game, his skills began to get noticed, and tales of his baseball ability spread across the Pacific Ocean to the California coast. [xxxi] The Sacramento Sacts, a baseball team in the Pacific Coast League, scouted Williams and signed him to a minor league contract in 1911 at the age of twenty-two. After being traded to a team in the Northwestern League, Williams experienced some moderate success that season, likely as a result of becoming accustomed to this higher level of competitive baseball. Williams rejoined the Sacramento team in 1912 and toured Hawaii with his new team. This created lots of excitement among Hawaiian baseball players and fans as their native son returned as a professional baseball player. In 1913, Williams won seventeen games against only seven losses for the Sacts and had an earned run average of just over 2.00. [xxxii] In addition to his pitching skills, stories from those who watched Williams play noted that his delivery to the mound was unusual and made it hard for batters to hit. This success on the mound was enough to create interest from several Major League baseball teams.

In 1914, Honolulu Johnny, as Williams had come to be known, was on the Major League roster of the Detroit Tigers. His first appearance as a Major League Baseball player was on April 21, 1914 when he was the starting pitcher for the Tigers against the Cleveland Indians. He only lasted one inning before being removed from the game by the Tigers' manager after he gave up several runs to the Indians. Although Williams did pitch in several more games that season for the Tigers, including pitching very well in a 3-0 loss to the great Walter "Big Train" Johnson and the Washington Senators. He finished his only Major League season with a record of zero wins and two losses, an inflated earned run average of 6.35, and four strikeouts. He gave up twelve runs and seventeen hits that season, in 11 1/3 innings of work. [xxxiii]

Throughout the 1914 season, Williams had been dealing with complications of apparent malaria, which had caused him setbacks during the year. By autumn of 1914, Honolulu Johnny was out of the major leagues and was pitching again with the Sacramento minor-league team, which would soon move to the bay area and become known as the San Francisco Missions. [xxxiv]

The significance of Johnny Williams in Major League Baseball cannot be overstated. At a time in the game when non-white players were not welcome in many areas of professional baseball, Williams was able to at least get a taste of the highest level of the game. It is particularly interesting that his teammate on the Tigers was Baseball Hall of Famer Ty Cobb, a southerner known as much for his alleged racism and bigotry as for his baseball prowess. "The Georgia Peach," as Cobb was known, was a legendary all-around player and a prolific hitter who held the all-time hits record in Major League baseball until 1985 when the record was broken by Cincinnati Reds' Pete Rose.

As great as the stories of Cobb's baseball records and exploits are, so too are the despicable stories of his disdain for people of color. Cobb was known to frequently use racial slurs and to propagate acts of hate toward blacks, Catholics, northerners, other people of color, and just about anyone who was different than Cobb himself. During his career, Cobb fought a black groundskeeper and choked the groundskeeper's wife. He stabbed a black night watchman who had stepped into an altercation in which Cobb slapped a black elevator operator for having what Cobb perceived as an arrogant attitude. He also brutally attacked a handicapped fan who had been heckling him. The fan had only one hand, and by some accounts, had no hands. Cobb was linked to an alleged "game fixing" scandal. [xxxv] Cobb made many enemies because of his treatment of other people, and when Cobb died in 1961, only four people who were connected to the game of baseball attended his funeral. [xxxvi] While it is true that later in life Cobb's stance on minorities began to soften publicly, this may have been the result of him being forced to a certain level of political correctness by a changing American society and an effort to promote a positive image for business purposes. People who have been evil and racist for most of their lives do not *usually* completely change their ways later in life.

Ty Cobb was a baseball superstar on the Detroit Tigers when Honolulu Johnny joined the team in 1914, and it is doubtful that he would have approved of a teammate who was not white. While there is no direct proof that Cobb made things rough for Williams or wanted him off the team, there is a story that can provide insight into his view. Hawaiians, like other Asian Pacific-Islanders had a somewhat exotic and novel place in western culture in the early 1900s, a viewpoint that was completely misguided and devoid of truth. A Detroit newspaper ran an article saying that Johnny Williams had gone without shoes until he was sixteen years old, and he could therefore use his feet just like his hands. [xxxvii] This was an obviously ridiculous statement. Hawaiian Major League Baseball player Henry "Hank" Oana once noted that people seemed to think that Hawaiians were "wild men of the woods." [xxxviii] Cobb was noted to be entertained by asking Honolulu Johnny to throw his luggage with his bare feet, something he would have likely not have asked of other white players and possibly an attempt to make fun of Williams or to ostracize him as being "different." This seems like a possible, if not probable, reality, at least to this author, considering Cobb's reputation and actions.

Williams would bounce around the minor leagues for a few more years but would never play Major League Baseball again. Honolulu Johnny later played on some Hawaiian touring baseball teams and later worked as a machinist, a trash collector, and dispatcher. He died in 1963 at the age of seventy-four. Though forgotten by many, Honolulu Johnny was the first person of Asian Pacific heritage to play in the big leagues.

The Prince

Before Jackie Robinson broke the Major League Baseball color barrier for all people, there would be three more native Hawaiians to play at baseball's highest level, although with a slight but interesting footnote. While Honolulu Johnny was born in the *Kingdom* of Hawaii, there was a brief four-year period after the kingdom fell and before it became a U.S. territory when Hawaii was an independent republic. It was during this period, in 1897, that Antone Do Rego was born on the Hawaiian island of Maui.

While Do Rego (who would later shorten his name to Tony Rego) was a native born Hawaiian, he was not of Asian or Pacific Islander descent. Rego's parents were both Portuguese immigrants to the Hawaiian Islands. Thousands of Portuguese came to Hawaii in the 1870s as the success of the sugar industry started to call for greater numbers of workers. The Portuguese influence on Hawaiian culture became significant, as did the Hawaiian influence on the Portuguese immigrants. This included a love for the game of baseball. [xxxix]

A right-handed hitting and right-handed throwing catcher, Rego made his Major League Baseball debut with the St. Louis Browns in June 1924 and played his last Major League Baseball game in September 1925. His career ended with a batting average of .286, no home runs, and eight runs batted in.

Although a native-born Hawaiian, Rego was considered white in Major League Baseball since both parents were European. [xl]

Another native-born Hawaiian had a similar background as Rego. Thomas Vardasco "Tony" Robello was born in Pahala, Hawaii in 1913. Like Rego, Robello's parents were of Portuguese descent. His father was a Portuguese immigrant from the Azores and his mother was the daughter of Portuguese immigrants. So while Robello was a native-born Hawaiian, he was not Asian Pacific Islander. [xli] Robello appeared in sixteen games in the Major Leagues as a second baseman and third baseman in 1933 and 1934 with the Cincinnati Reds, finishing his career with a batting average of .219, no home runs, three doubles, one run, and three RBI. [xlii] His reputation, however, was made not as a player, but as a baseball scout. He is credited as helping to build the 1975 and 1976 Cincinnati Reds team, known as the Big Red Machine that won back-to-back World Series championships.

The other native-born Hawaiian to play Major League Baseball before 1947 was Henry Kawaihoa Oana, Jr.. "Hank" was born in Waipahu, Hawaii on January 22, 1910. [xliii] Hank's father was native Hawaiian, and his mother was of Portuguese descent. In fact, in a time when many dark-skinned players were not welcome to Major League Baseball, the fact that Hank's mother was European was later used as a selling point for acceptance in the big leagues.

Like many Hawaiian boys of his era, Oana grew up playing baseball on sugar plantations. An all-around athlete, Oana had exceptional interest in baseball and grew up playing in leagues around the islands. There are differing accounts of Oana's entry into professional baseball, with some giving Ty Cobb credit for "discovering" Oana. There is little to no evidence to support this notion, and given Cobb's well-known racism and bigotry toward dark-skinned people, it is at best, unlikely. Oana's own account of how he began his career did not include any mention of Ty Cobb. [xliv]

Oana came to California to seek success in professional baseball in 1928 and worked as a dockworker in the San Francisco Bay area through the week, while playing in a local winter league on the weekends. He was able to make the opening day roster for the San Francisco Seals that next spring. The Seals were a minor league baseball team based in San Francisco at the time; they played in the Pacific Coast League and were not affiliated with any Major League Baseball team when Oana was there in the late 1920s. However, the club determined that he needed more work on his defensive skills and sent him down to a lower affiliate in Arizona. By the middle of the 1930 season, Hank was recalled to the Seals and became a starting outfielder for San Francisco, due primarily to his effectiveness at the plate. Oana experienced a great deal of success in the Pacific Coast League until his performance began to decline in 1932. [xlv] Some accounts attribute this to an old football injury that was causing vision problems, while other accounts note that Oana had begun to experience difficulties with alcohol and was enjoying the late-night party scene in San Francisco. Vince DiMaggio would replace Oana as the Seals' starting centerfielder in the later part of the 1932 season. [xlvi] In 1933, after an incident at a San Francisco nightclub, Hank was released by the Seals and became part of the Portland Beavers baseball club, a Pacific Coast League rival of San Francisco. Oana turned his fortune around in Portland and had a productive 1933 season, while Portland won the Pacific Coast League championship. Before the 1933 season, Oana sought medical help for his vision problems and turned around his extracurricular behavior. It is not a coincidence that both of these coincided with his return to return to prominence in the PCL. It is at this this point that the nickname "Prince" started to be associated with Hank Oana, as stories circulated that he Hawaiian royalty. There is scant evidence for this claim, and Oana himself even dismissed it as a publicity stunt by the Portland Beavers.[xlvii] However, the nickname stuck, and many people insisted on believing the story of his royal heritage.

Oana's big break came in 1934 when the Philadelphia Phillies picked up his contract from Portland. Hank was an outfielder for the Phillies and made his Major League Baseball debut on April 22, 1934. Oana would go on to appear in just six games for Philadelphia in 1934, and he finished the season with a .238 batting average in twenty-one at-bats. He had a double, three runs batted in, and scored three runs that season while playing the outfield without any errors.[xlviii] Once Oana was sent back to Portland, his contract was quickly sold to a minor league team in Atlanta, where Hank would encounter some racial intolerance due to his dark skin. Oana had a great deal of success with the Atlanta Crackers, and the manager of the Southern Association team said that one of his reasons for bringing Oana to Atlanta was "we needed a hero for colored citizens."[xlix] One Atlanta newspaper repeatedly reported that Oana himself was black, which, in the opinion of the newspaper, was unacceptable.[l] Oana bounced around various levels of the minor leagues for several years thereafter, including stints with the Syracuse Chiefs, Knoxville, Little Rock, Hickory, Jackson, and finally Fort Worth. It was there that Oana started to experience an unlikely return to the Major Leagues. In 1942, Fort Worth manager (and Baseball Hall of Famer) Rogers Hornsby noted that Oana's hitting was not very good and compared it to the hitting ability of a pitcher. Hank then told him that he was a pitcher as a kid growing up in Hawaii and had studied pitching over the years in his minor league career. Even though he had pitched in limited instances in the minors, it was Hornsby who gave him the opportunity to carve out a niche on the mound at the age of thirty-two. Oana experienced a great deal of success as a pitcher in Fort Worth that year, ending the season with a record of sixteen wins and five losses, a very impressive earned run average of 1.72, with three shutouts and a no-hitter.[li] His newfound success as a pitcher led him back the Major Leagues in 1943 with the Detroit Tigers, nine years after he had last played in the big leagues.

He appeared in ten games and had a record of three wins and two losses with the Tigers that year, along with an ERA of 4.50. He also had twenty-six at-bats, hitting .385 with one home run and seven RBI. Hank spent 1944 in the minor leagues with Buffalo, but briefly returned to the Tigers in 1945, appearing in three games, with one start, no record, an ERA of 1.59, and one hit in five at-bats.[lii] Oana played several more years in the minor leagues, had several operations on his eyes, went on to work in a rehabilitation center for people who were blind, and operated a fishing business. The "Prince" died in 1976 at the age of sixty-six from ongoing heart problems.[liii]

Summary

Honolulu Johnny and the Prince helped bring diversity to Major League Baseball many years before Jackie Robinson officially brought integration to the game, when only a few Latin American and Native American players were allowed to play at the game's highest level. Although their contributions to the game are often unrecognized, these men overcame stereotypes and intolerance to carve out their place in baseball history and to pave the way for other Asian Pacific Americans in Major League

Baseball, taking their place with other heroes of the pre-integration era.

Pitching Statistics for Chapter Three

Player	WL %	ERA	Saves	Wins	Losses	Strike outs	Walks	Innings Pitched
Williams, John	0	6.35	0	0	2	4	5	11.1
Oana, Henry	0.6	3.77	1	3	2	18	26	45.1

Batting Statistics for Chapter Three

Player	Runs	Hits	BA	On Base %	RBI	H R	Stolen Bases	Plate Appearances
Oana, Henry	8	16	0.308	0.321	10	1	0	53

Chapter Four

Bobby Balcena: The Asian-American Jackie Robinson

Introduction

In 2013, at an Asian-Pacific American Heritage Month event in Chicago, Illinios, former Illinois Governor Pat Quinn III claimed that Bobby Balcena is the 'Jackie Robinson' of Asians in the Major League. [liv] Bobby Balcena is a name that was, and remains, unknown to many people, even in baseball circles. Early baseball was filled with attempts to circumvent the pre-Jackie Robinson era color barrier, so some information is vague regarding early major league baseball players and their ethnicity or background. While we have discussed two Hawaiian-born players who played in Major League Baseball earlier, many consider the former Cincinnati Redleg (Reds) Outfielder, Bobby Balcena, to be the first Asian Pacific American to play Major League Baseball.

Bobby Balcena

"Our Game Too"

Bobby Balcena

(Photos Courtesy of the Cincinnati Reds)

The son of immigrants from the Philippines, Robert Rudolph Balcena, known as Bobby, was born August 1, 1925 in San Pedro, California. Balcena attended San Pedro High School (Rolling Hills Prep) and was an excellent baseball and football player. Balcena played for the Cincinnati Redlegs from September 16 to September 29, 1956. [lv] Balcena is quoted as saying, "I wasn't up there long. But I was there." [lvi] Balcena was also the first Filipino American to make it to the Major Leagues. [lvii] Bobby was a right-handed hitting, left-handed throwing outfielder who weighed 160 pounds and stood five feet and seven inches tall. The Seattle Times noted that Balcena's strong upper body gave him lots of pop with the bat. When in Seattle, he had asked the team to install a chin-up bar in the training room and would complete a hundred chin-ups with ease. This was at a time when strength training was not a common practice in baseball. Balcena was a brilliant defensive player who was also admired for his speed and hustle on the base paths. While his brief career in the Major Leagues with the Reds produced just two at-bats and two runs in seven games, his illustrious minor-league career lasted fifteen years and made him somewhat of a baseball icon in the Seattle area, as well as among Filipino-American communities.

Balcena's career in professional baseball began in 1948 with Mexicali Aquilas (Baja California, Mexico) in the Sunset League, a "Class C" league. Balcena, a young man of only twenty-two, appeared in 102 games, with eight home runs and hit .369. Balcena led the Sunset League in hitting, and earned a spot on the Sunset League All-Star team as a rookie. In 1950, Balcena broke into the MLB-affiliated minor leagues in the United States with the Western League's Wichita Indians, a single "A" affiliate of the St. Louis Browns. Balcena hit .290 that season, and over the next three seasons progressed as high as "AAA" in the Browns' farm system before being traded to the New York Yankees organization before the start of the 1954 season. By 1955, Balcena was out of MLB affiliated minor league baseball and was playing for the Seattle Raniers in the Pacific Coast League.

After hitting over .290 for two seasons with the Raniers, Balcena's breakthrough to Major League Baseball finally happened in 1956. The Cincinnati Redlegs promoted Balcena from Seattle, a new Cincinnati Redlegs AAA affiliate to help in

48

the 1956 National League pennant chase. Balcena's first major league game was at Ebbets Field against the Brooklyn Dodgers, the same team that baseball hall of famer Jackie Robinson had played for when he broke baseball's color barrier in 1947. Balcena was thirty years old when he debuted for Cincinnati and appeared in the game as a pinch hitter as the Redlegs lost 3-2 to Brooklyn. After a combined seven games played for Cincinnati in 1956, Balcena received an invitation to spring training by the Reds but would never reach the Major Leagues again. Balcena played AAA baseball in the minor leagues with various organizations until he finished his baseball career in 1962 with the Minnesota Twins AAA Vancouver team in the Pacific Coast League at age thirty-eight. While Bobby Balcena's statistics in Major League Baseball were sparse due to his brief stay in Cincinnati, his minor league statistics over fifteen seasons were noteworthy. Balcena appeared in 2,018 games, scored 685 runs, gathered an impressive 2,019 hits, including 134 Home Runs and 441 Runs Batted In, and had a .282 batting average!

During his lengthy career in professional baseball, Bobby "The Filipino Flyer" Balcena was one of the most popular players in the Pacific Coast League, as fans appreciated his enthusiastic style of play, easy smile, and engaging personality. Bobby's locker in Seattle was usually near the training room door, and he was friendly with everyone who came through. He also gave away some of his game-used gear to fans, and the kids loved him. His affection for the Seattle area continued even after he was traded by the Raniers, as he often returned to the Seattle area each winter and rented a fishing cabin on a nearby lake. After his baseball playing days were over, Bobby made a living for a time as a schoolteacher. He returned home in the mid-1960s to San Pedro, California where he worked as a longshoreman for many years. He died January 5, 1990 in San Pedro, California of natural causes while watching television in his favorite chair. The town of San Pedro had a celebration of their hometown hero after his death.

Many have forgotten the contributions of Robert Rudolph Balcena to baseball over the decades, but it was his enthusiasm, demeanor, talent, and love for this game that helped him break new barriers in Major League Baseball and further the cause of equality in America's pastime. Perhaps Bobby was loved so much by fans because of his friendly, unassuming nature; or because he played every game like he was having fun and loved to play; or because maybe fans, regardless of skin tone or ethnicity, could see a little bit of themselves in Bobby Balcena, who persevered against the odds to achieve his dream.

Summary

Many baseball historians regard Bobby Balcena as the first Asian Pacific-American player in Major League Baseball. Balcena's MLB career was brief; however, he had an impressive minor league professional career before retiring. Balcena is remembered as a player who played the game with love and intensity, usually with a smile on his face, and as a man who was great ambassador for baseball, loved by fans in the baseball towns he called home. The next chapter will include profiles of Asian Pacific-American baseball players in the 1960s, as well as a profile of the first Japanese-born player in Major League Baseball.

Bobby Balcena Batting Statistics

Player	Runs	Hits	BA	On Base %	RBI	HR	Stolen Bases	Plate Appearances
Balcena, Bobby	2	0	0	0	0	0	0	2

Chapter Five

The 1960s

Introduction

The 1960s in baseball, as with American culture on the whole, was a time of change and reform. The decade brought expansion to Major League Baseball and took the big leagues to new geographical areas, including Canada. As movements increased to demand rights and equality in the country, the MLB players union was formed and would leave an imprint that would forever change the game. Fidel Castro seized power in the baseball-crazy island nation of Cuba; his communism meant a drastic change for Cuban baseball players coming to the United States and the loss of Havana as a part of minor league baseball.[lviii] The controversial Ty Cobb, baseball's all-time hits leader at the time, died during this decade, as did Branch Rickey who was so instrumental in bringing Jackie Robinson in the major leagues. Roger Maris' great chase to break Babe Ruth's single season home run record dominated the 1960s. In 1968, Red Sox outfielder Carl Yastremzki won baseball's Triple Crown, something no one else would be able to do until 2012. While Mike Lum is the only player in this chapter born in the United States, two other players are noteworthy for their accomplishments in the 1960s. Masanori Murakami was the first player from Japan to play Major League Baseball, and Tony Solaita, born in American Samoa (a United States territory), also broke through to baseball's highest level.

Masanori Murakami

(Photo courtesy of the Baseball Hall of Fame and Museum)

While Masanori Murakami was not Asian Pacific-American, he is noteworthy because he was the first Japanese-born player in the MLB. [lix] He was a pioneer for the many Japanese born and Asian born players who would continue to make an impact on American baseball for decades. Interestingly, it could have been Hiroshi Takahashi or Tatsuhiko Tanaka who broke through as the first Japanese born player in MLB history. The mid-1960s saw an influx of Japanese immigrants into the United States due to the Immigration Act of 1965. The San Francisco Bay area already had a large Japanese population, and removal of these immigration quotas increased that population. Like many Americans at the time, Japanese immigrants were in love with the game of baseball. So it made sense from a financial and popularity standpoint that the local San Francisco Giants would want to capitalize by bringing in baseball players from Japan. In 1964, the Giants signed Hiroshi Takahashi, a catcher; Tatsuhiko Tanaka, an infielder; and Masanori Murakami, a left-handed pitcher to minor league contracts. All three of the players were in their late teens at the time. [lx] Murakami was better developed in his baseball skill than the other two young Japanese players and was assigned to the Giants' farm team in Fresno of the single A California League. Murakami was born May 6, 1944 in Yamanashi, Japan. He had previously pitched professionally for the Nankai Hawks in the Japan Pacific League (of Nippon Professional Baseball) before arriving in the United States. Relying primarily on a fastball and curve ball, Murakami went 11-7 for the Giants' team in Fresno with an impressive 1.78 Earned Run Average, and later that same year, he made his MLB debut on September 1, 1964 for the San Francisco Giants. He received a standing ovation from the crowd of 40,000+ at New York's Shea Stadium that day as the Giants played the Mets. [lxi] He appeared in nine games for San Francisco that autumn, going 1-0, with an ERA of 1.80, and picked up a save. Murakami would return to the Giants again in 1965, going 4-1 in forty-five appearances (almost all in relief), with an ERA of 3.75 while picking up eight saves. Murakami had certainly proven his ability to pitch successfully at the Major League level in the United

States, and to many MLB fans, this bolstered their opinion of the Japanese Pacific League, which had been considered by many Americans to only be at a mid-minor league level. Murakami's success caused them to rethink that notion. The positive change Murakami's success brought about regarding the way Japanese leagues and players were perceived by Major League baseball cannot be overstated. Despite his success in the United States and his great popularity in the San Francisco area and across the country, the young player missed his family in Japan, became homesick, and had decided to remain in Japan when he returned home after the 1964 season. But due to a contract dispute, the Japanese league and MLB compromised that he would pitch the 1965 season in San Francisco and then return to Nippon Professional Baseball to continue his career.[lxii] Murakami played his final MLB game on October 1, 1965. His career MLB win-loss percentage was .833, winning five games and losing one. Appearing in fifty-four games, Murakami had 100 strikeouts and nine saves.[lxiii] He would go on to play eighteen more seasons in Japan, and actually attempted a comeback in professional baseball in the United States with the Giants organization in 1983. At age thirty-eight, however, he was unsuccessful in his bid to return to Major League Baseball. Following Masanori's success and popularity in Major League Baseball, the Japanese professional leagues became much more protective over their players and valued them more. It would be three decades before another Japanese born player made it to Major League Baseball, Hideo Nomo in 1995.[lxiv]

"Our Game Too"

Tony Solaita

Tolia Solaita (Tony) was born January 15, 1947 in Nuuuli, America Samoa. America Samoa became a territory of the United States in the nineteenth century, and people born there are considered U.S. Nationals with the right to hold U.S. Passports. The question of official U.S. citizenship for American Samoans is being considered in the United States court system as of the writing of this book. Solaitia, like many American Samoan kids, grew up playing kirikiti, a Samoan game closely related to cricket, as attempts by American soldiers to promote baseball in the islands never gained much traction. It was not until 1955, at the age of eight, that he was introduced to baseball when his family moved to Hawaii as his father joined the United States Marines. [lxv] His family later moved to California where Tony attended high school and excelled at both baseball and football, eventually giving up football to focus on high school baseball as a pitcher and first baseman. It was the power hitting potential of Solaita that attracted attention from professional scouts, and he was signed as an amateur free agent by the Yankees organization in 1965. [lxvi]

In 1968, he was named the Topps Minor League Player of the Year after hitting fifty-one home runs with the Yankees single-A team in the Carolina League; he later made his Major League Baseball debut on September 16, 1968 with the New York Yankees. Solaita, the slugger who once won a home run contest over several baseball legends, including Mickey Mantle and Carl Yastrzemski, would not appear again in the Major Leagues until 1974 with the Kansas City Royals. [lxvii] Tony, whose father had become a Christian minister, went on to have a productive seven-year career in the big leagues, playing for the New Yankees, Kansas City Royals, California Angels, Montreal

Expos, and Toronto Blue Jays. [lxviii] Solaita ranked twenty-first in the American League in homeruns during the 1975 season, with a total of sixteen homeruns. [lxix] His attitude, friendliness, fierce competitiveness, and professionalism made him a team-favorite and a fan-favorite wherever he played, and in the autumn of his 1976 season with the Angels, the team held a Samoan heritage night at the ballpark, which was attended by tens of thousands of people from the Samoan community in the Los Angeles area. [lxx]

Tony played his final MLB game on September 30, 1979 and remains the only player born in American Samoa to play Major League Baseball. Tony went on to play four more seasons in the Japanese Pacific League with the Nippon Ham Fighters, averaging thirty-nine home runs and ninety-three runs batted in per season in Japan. Solaita retired permanently from baseball in 1984 at age thirty-seven. He was murdered at age forty-three on February 10, 1990 in Tafuna, American Samoa while trying to confront a person who had been vandalizing his neighborhood, business, and property. [lxxi]

"Our Game Too"

Tony Solaita

(Photo Courtesy of Bryan Kuhn Photo Archives)

"Our Game Too"

Mike Lum

Michael Ken-Wai Lum was born October 7, 1945 in Honolulu, Hawaii. Lum is of Japanese and Hawaiian ancestry, but identified as Chinese-Hawaiian.[lxxii] Lum grew up playing baseball in Hawaii and developed a love for the game, but he excelled at both baseball and football as teenager. While also attracting the attention of baseball scouts, Lum was a high school football star at Roosevelt High School in Honolulu and was named the Interscholastic League of Honolulu's "Back of the Year" in 1962 as a left-handed quarterback. This led to a football scholarship offer from Brigham Young University in Utah, which Lum accepted. He decided, however, to give up college football at Brigham Young to sign a professional baseball contract with the Milwaukee Braves of the National League in 1963. [lxxiii]

Lum was assigned to the Braves single-A farm team in Waycross, Georgia and he experienced quite a culture shock from his native Hawaii, primarily when encountering the racism of the Deep South and the unfair treatment of African-American players. [lxxiv] Lum made his MLB debut on September 12, 1967 for the Atlanta Braves. Lum spent fifteen years in the league, playing for the Atlanta Braves, Cincinnati Reds, and Chicago Cubs. He played his final MLB game on September 30, 1981.[lxxv]

Lum achieved several noteworthy honors and distinctions during his career. He was on base when his Braves teammate Hammerin' Hank Aaron hit his 714th home run to tie the legendary Babe Ruth as baseball's all-time home run king on April 4, 1974 in Cincinnati. [lxxvi] He was also the third of only six players to ever pinch hit for Hank Aaron. [lxxvii] On July 3, 1970, Lum hit three homeruns in one game for the Atlanta Braves, a rare feat in baseball history. In 1973, Lum ranked eleventh among National League players in triples with six triples, and was fifteenth in batting average with a cumulative average of .294. [lxxviii] Lum was traded to the World Series Champion Cincinnati Reds in 1976 and was a member of the 1976 World Series team. Lum played in the postseason playoffs for Cincinnati but not the World Series. [lxxix] The starting members of the "Big Red Machine" dominated the lineup during much of the World Series, but Lum's contributions to the team's success were significant throughout the season. Lum played alongside baseball hall of famers Pete Rose, Johnny Bench, Tony Perez, Joe Morgan and Tom Seaver during his tenure in Cincinnati from 1976-1978.

In 2016, the 1976 Reds World Championship team was honored at an on-field ceremony at the Great American Ballpark in Cincinnati, and Lum walked on to the field to a standing ovation by Reds fans in appreciation of his contributions to the iconic 1976 team on the fortieth anniversary of this title. While Lum had received more playing time in Atlanta than Cincinnati, he embraced the trade to the Reds as an opportunity to play for a winning team and win a championship. Lum was one of the players in the trade that Reds manager Sparky Anderson coveted as a key component in the Reds continued championship efforts, as Lum provided good defense in the outfield, could play first base, and had gained a reputation as a solid left-handed hitter off the bench. [lxxx] Lum is renowned as one of the great pinch-hitters in baseball history and actually led the National League in pinch-hits in 1979, hitting an impressive .326 as a pinch hitter that season. He finished his career with 103 pinch hits, seventeenth all-time. [lxxxi]

Since retiring from playing in the MLB, Lum has remained active in baseball. In 1982, Lum played one season for the Yokohama Taiyo Whales of the Japan Central League (Nippon Pro Baseball), hitting .269 with twelve home runs and forty-six runs batted in. Lum served as hitting coach, instructor, and hitting coordinator for the Chicago White Sox, Kansas City Royals, and Milwaukee Brewers. In 2010, Lum joined the coaching staff of the Pittsburgh Pirates organization as a hitting instructor.[lxxxii] An interesting note is that when Michael Jordan, perhaps the greatest basketball player of all-time, decided to leave the game and attempt a career in professional baseball in the mid-1990s, it was Mike Lum who was his hitting coach in the White Sox organization.[lxxxiii]

Mike Lum

(Photo courtesy of the Cincinnati Reds)

"Our Game Too"

Mike Lum

(Photo courtesy of the Cincinnati Reds)

"Our Game Too"

Mike Lum

(Photo courtesy of the Cincinnati Reds)

Summary

The 1960s witnessed several firsts in the MLB for Asian and Asian Pacific-American Players. There was the debut of Mike Lum, who was the first Asian Pacific-American player to later go on to win a World Series, and then Masanori Murakami was the first Japanese born player in the MLB. Tragically, Tony Solaita's life was cut short by unnecessary violence. While this chapter highlighted the accomplishments of the first Japanese MLB player and early Asian Pacific-American pioneers in the MLB, the following chapter explores players who increased the impact of Asian Pacific Americans in the game throughout the 1970s.

Batting Statistics for MLB Players in the 1960s

Player	Runs	Hits	BA	On Base %	RBI	HR	Stolen Bases	Plate Appearances
Lum, Mike	404	877	0.24 7	0.31 9	431	90	13	4001
Solaita, Tony	164	336	0.255	0.35 7	203	50	2	1554

Chapter Six

The 1970s

Introduction

This decade was an addendum to the previous decade in the continued fight for equality and the struggle to be heard by many groups on a variety of issues, including the Vietnam War. While some Americans found meaning in counter-culture movements, others struggled to define and redefine "American" values. The early 1970s in baseball saw the death of baseball heroes Roberto Clemente and Jackie Robinson, losses that would be felt throughout the game. George Steinbrenner purchased the Yankees, which would go on to impact the way money was spent by big market teams for decades to come. Additionally, the designated hitter became part of Major League Baseball, at least for half of MLB. Baseball fans were sharply divided then, as they are now, by the DH rule and the emergence of "Mr. October." The "Big Red Machine" of Cincinnati would be considered the greatest team ever assembled by some, but Yankees fans would disagree. With formal U.S.-Cuba relations at a standstill, the Caribbean nation of the Dominican Republic would take its place as an island hotbed of baseball talent. In American politics, Richard Nixon and Watergate would change the way Americans viewed the Presidency, and Hank Aaron would eclipse the career home run record of the great Babe Ruth. The country was changing, and baseball was changing with it. Chapter Seven explores the tumultuous decade of the 1970s in baseball and focuses on the careers of several more Asian Pacific-American baseball players, and one memorable coach. These include: Wendell Kim, Len Sakata, Milt Wilcox, and Ryan Kurosaki.

"Our Game Too"

Wendell Kim

(Photo Courtesy of the Boston Red Sox)

Wendell Kealohepauloe Kim was born March 9, 1950 in Honolulu, Hawaii, and was raised near Long Beach, California where his family moved so his father could pursue a boxing career. Kim was of Korean and Hawaiian descent. Kim was signed by the San Francisco Giants as a free agent in 1973 but only made it to the Triple A level of baseball after eight seasons. Although he never actually played Major League Baseball, Kim made many contributions to the MLB, mainly as an iconic first base and third base coach. Kim is often credited as being the first Korean-American to wear a Major League uniform, albeit not as a player. Kim coached first and third bases for the San Francisco Giants from 1989 to 1996. Later, he coached third base for the Boston Red Sox from 1997 to 2000, and for the Chicago Cubs during the 2003 and 2004 seasons. He served as the bench coach for the Montreal Expos in 2002. Kim also managed minor league teams for the San Francisco Giants, Milwaukee Brewers, and Washington Nationals organization. [lxxxiv]   Wendell was affectionately nicknamed "Wave 'em in Wendell" by many fans due to his aggressive coaching style in which he would often send runners home as they rounded third base, in even the worst of situations. He was as likely to be met with thunderous applause as he was with a round of "boos," but the fans loved him just about everywhere he went, and he loved them back. In was not unusual for Wendell to take the time to talk baseball with just about anyone, and he was always willing to share his knowledge to help his players or team.

Wendell Kim had overcome a troubled childhood in which his father was abusive to Wendell and his siblings and beat his mother. Wendell's father was murdered when Wendell was just eight years old. [lxxxv] Wendell threw himself into baseball and education, working hard as a player and a student. He played high school baseball in the Los Angeles area and become an all-league player at California State Polytechnic University in Pomona. He was signed by the San Francisco Giants organization as a free agent in 1973 and assigned to the Giants single-A team in Decatur, Illinois of the Midwest League. [lxxxvi] During Kim's minor league career as a player, he hit .285 with 630 hits, and 208 RBI in 628 games while primarily playing the infield. Although he was the manager for several minor league teams in his career, "Wave em' in Wendell" is best remembered and loved for his passion, style, and accountability as a third base coach in the Major Leagues.

Despite his tough childhood experiences, Wendell Kim overcame these obstacles and chose a path of hard work, positivity, and love in both his career and family life, leaving a wonderful legacy as a kind man who sought to make a difference. [lxxxvii] Kim co-authored *Youth Baseball: A Coach's and Parent's Guide (The Art & Science of Coaching Series)* with Sally Tippett-Rains, focusing on instruction, motivation, and advice for those involved in youth baseball. The book was published in 1997 by Sport Publishing.[lxxxviii] Kim retired from the game in 2005 when he began to suffer memory loss from the early onset of Alzheimer's disease. His condition worsened significantly in the years to come, and he passed away on February 15, 2015 in Phoenix, Arizona.

Lenn Sakata

Lenn Haruki Sakata was born June 8, 1954 in Honolulu, Hawaii and is Japanese-American. He grew up playing baseball in the Honolulu area and attended Kalani High School. It was there that he played on the same team as Ryan Kurosaki, who would also go on to play Major League Baseball. Sakata was originally drafted by the San Francisco Giants, but he decided to remain in college, eventually ending up at Gonzaga University, where he was a second-team All-American infielder. Sakata would again be drafted by another major league team, and he would forgo the draft to remain in school again. He finally decided to sign with a major league team after being drafted by the Milwaukee Brewers in 1975. Sakata progressed quickly through the Milwaukee farm system and made his MLB debut July 21, 1977 for the Brewers.[lxxxix] Sakata remained with the Brewers organization for a few years, being shipped back and forth between the big league team and their AAA affiliate in Spokane (and later Vancouver) mostly due to his inconsistency at the plate. Sakata was traded to the Baltimore Orioles before the 1980 season and began that season with the Orioles affiliate in Rochester where he hit .344 in twenty-six games, enough to earn a call-up to the big league team. Sakata would remain in the Major Leagues with the Orioles for the better part of the next six seasons. After the Orioles did not offer him a contract after the 1985 season, Sakata went on to play with the Oakland Athletics and New York Yankees before retiring in late 1987.

There were several highlights in Sakata's eleven years as a player in the MLB.[xc] Sakata was mostly used as a utility player during his career, and even famously served as an emergency catcher in the top of the tenth inning on August 24, 1983 with the Orioles. Surviving the top of the inning, Sakata hit a three run homerun in the bottom of the tenth inning to win the game. That same year, Sakata's Orioles won the World Series as well.[xci] Sakata was also the last Oriole to regularly play the position of shortstop before baseball hall of fame Shortstop/Third Baseman Cal Ripken, Jr. began his legendary record-breaking iron-man streak with the team. In 2000, Sakata reflected on his days playing in the MLB, saying: "Baseball provides a great learning experience in human relations. People come from all over the world and live together with one common link: The love of baseball."[xcii] He played for the Milwaukee Brewers, Baltimore Orioles, New York Yankees, and Oakland Athletics.[xciii]

Sakata coached in MLB, and managed in both the minor leagues and Japan. Sakata worked for the Oakland Athletics organization from 1988-1990 and for the California Angels from 1991 to 1994. Sakata managed in the San Francisco Giants minor leagues from 1999 to 2007 and in the Oakland A's organization from 1988 to 1989 (winning Northwest League Manager of the Year in 1988). Notably, Sakata managed three California League Championships during his tenure as manager. In Japan, Sakata managed the Chiba Lotte Marines and the Nippon Professional teams. In 2011, Sakata returned the US to coach in the Colorado Rockies minor league system. In 2014, he returned to the Giants' organization.[xciv] Sakata's continued presence as a coach and manager in the MLB have earned him accolades from his peers. One of which was earning the CAL Manager of the Year in 2005. [xcv]

"Our Game Too"

Lenn Sakata

(Photo Courtesy of Bryan Kuhn Photo Archives)

"Our Game Too"

Milt Wilcox

Milton Edward Wilcox was born April 20, 1950 in Honolulu, Hawaii. His father was of indigenous Hawaiian ancestry. Milt's family moved to Oklahoma when he was very young, and he was drafted by the Cincinnati Reds organization in the second round of the 1968 amateur draft. After success in the Reds minor leagues with Tampa and Indianapolis, Wilcox made an impact when he was promoted. He made his MLB debut September 5, 1970 for the Cincinnati Reds, who were in the middle of a pennant chase. Milt went 3-1 with the Reds that fall, throwing a complete game and a shutout with an ERA of just 2.42; he helped the Reds win the 1970 National League West title and went on to play for the Reds in the National League Championship Series and the World Series, which they lost to the Baltimore Orioles. He would not appear again in the postseason until 1984 with the Detroit Tigers. Wilcox pitched again for Cincinnati (both AAA and the big league team) in 1971 before being traded to the Cleveland Indians after the season. [xcvi]

Wilcox spent the next few years with the Indians, as well as one season with the Chicago Cubs organization while battling illnesses and arm pain, before finding an MLB home with the Detroit Tigers in 1977. It is as a Tiger, that Milt Wilcox is best remembered and had the most success. After his initial season with the Tigers in 1977, when he went 6-2, Wilcox posted double digit wins with the club for the next seven seasons, culminating with a career year in 1984 in which he went 17-8. [xcvii] In the 1984 postseason, Wilcox went 2-0 in the American League Championship Series and the World Series. In the ALCS against the Kansas City Royals, Wilcox had an ERA of 0, and in the 1984 World Series against the San Diego Padres, Wilcox had an ERA of 1.50. With Wilcox, the Tigers defeated the Padres to become

World Series Champions. [xcviii] Wilcox suffered shoulder problems, which limited his contributions in the 1985 season. After which, he filed for free agency. At age thirty-six, he spent the 1986 season with the Seattle Mariners, appearing in thirteen games and going 0-8. It would be his final season in Major League Baseball. He finished his MLB career with 119 wins. Wilcox threw a near perfect game on April 15, 1983 against the Chicago White Sox. [xcix] Jerry Hairston hit a single with two outs in the ninth inning to break up the perfect game, but the Tigers won the game 6-0, and Wilcox was named American League Player of the Week. [c]

During his sixteen years pitching in the MLB, Wilcox played for the Cincinnati Reds, Detroit Tigers, Cleveland Indians, Chicago Cubs, and Seattle Mariners, and earned a spot on several MLB leaderboards. In 1978, Wilcox ranked tenth in the American League in Strikeout/Walk Ration with 1.94, seventh in complete games with sixteen, and he also ranked eighth in Strikeouts per Nine Innings with 5.52. In 1981, he ranked seventh in Wins in the American League with a total of twelve. In 1984, Wilcox ranked fourth in the American League with a winning percentage of .680, and he ranked sixth in Wins with a total of seventeen. [ci]

After retiring, Wilcox worked as a youth baseball instructor and broadcaster for a while. He started a company called Ultimate Air Dogs where he trains dogs to perform dock jumping at events around the country. [cii] He founded the business in 2002. [ciii]

"Our Game Too"

Ryan Kurosaki

Ryan Yoshitomo Kurosaki was born July 3, 1952 in Honolulu, Hawaii. Ryan attended American Japanese Association baseball games with his dad while he was growing up and played the game as much as possible. Kurosaki played on the high school baseball team at Kalani High School in Honolulu with another future MLB player, Lenn Sakata. That 1970 team went on to win the state baseball championship in Hawaii. [civ] Kurosaki was awarded a baseball scholarship to the University of Nebraska, and in 1974, he was signed to his first professional contract by the St. Louis Cardinals organization. He was assigned to the Cardinals single-A team in Modesto of the California League, and in 1975, was promoted to the Cardinals' Arkansas team where he was one of the top relief pitchers in the AA Texas League. By mid-year, he had been called up to the Major Leagues. He made his MLB debut May 20, 1975 for the St. Louis Cardinals at age twenty-two, playing on the same team with Hall of Famers Lou Brock and Bob Gibson. Kurosaki appeared in seven games for the Cardinals, in what would be his only Major League season. He had a 0-0 record, with a 7.62 Earned Run Average. [cv] His final MLB game was June 16, 1975, after which he was sent back to the Cardinals AA team in Arkansas and spent the next few years in various levels of the Cardinals minor-league system until his professional baseball career ended after the 1980 season. Kurosaki's stay in the Major Leagues was brief, but it was important. He is credited as the first Japanese-American to play Major League Baseball. [cvi] "I was just blessed to become the first person of my ancestry to reach the big leagues," Kurosaki later noted. [cvii] But Kurosaki says that he never thought much about the significance of what he accomplished at the time, "When you get on the field, it's basically you competing against

73

the competition. I really didn't have time to think about it."[cviii] After baseball, Ryan Kurosaki and his family eventually made their home in Arkansas where he worked as a firefighter.

Summary

Most of the Asian Pacific-American influence in the 1970s came from the state of Hawaii, the American state with the highest Asian Pacific-American population. Hawaii's multicultural way of life and deep-rooted love for the game of baseball fostered the development of many young players. Wendell Kim, who never actually played in the big leagues, would make his impact as a coach, helping nurture others in their career and contributing to his team in whatever way possible. While he never played MLB, he also helped break down barriers for Asian Pacific-Americans in the coaching aspect of the game. The 1970s saw a young infielder from Hawaii, Lenn Sakata, whose versatility would become his trademark and two pitchers, Wilcox and Kurosaki, whose careers would be for very different durations but both historically noteworthy.

Pitching Statistics for the 1970s

Player	WL %	ERA	Saves	Wins	Losses	Strikeouts	Walks	Innings Pitched
Wilcox, Milt	0.513	4.07	6	119	113	1137	770	2016.2
Kurosaki, Ryan	0	7.62	0	0	0	6	7	13

"Our Game Too"

Batting Statistics for the 1970s

Player	Runs	Hits	BA	On Base %	RBI	HR	Stolen Bases	Plate Appearances
Sakata, Lenn	163	296	0.23	0.286	109	25	30	1423

Chapter Seven

The 1980s

Introduction

The 1980s in Major League Baseball began on a sour note with the first baseball players' strike in 1981, which brought the game to a standstill for several weeks. After the game's first work stoppage, a decade of labor uncertainty followed. Just four years later, a kid from Cincinnati would break one of the most seemingly untouchable and sacred records in the game when Pete Rose passed Ty Cobb to become baseball's all-time hit king. Meanwhile in Boston, the Sox seemed on the verge of finally breaking the "Curse of the Bambino" in 1986. The Red Sox last won a World Series in 1918, but sold the Hall of Famer to their arch-rival, the New York Yankees in December 1919. The opportunity to break the curse in 1986, however, would be lost. Whether fair or unfair, the poster boy for the loss would be Red Sox first baseman Billy Buckner, one of the best defensive first basemen in the game at the time. A softly hit ground ball from the Mets' Mookie Wilson trickled through his legs for an error. In American politics and culture, the decade gave rise to new conservative movement in the country that would see former Hollywood actor Ronald Reagan become the U.S. President, meanwhile the first woman would be appointed to the United States Supreme Court, and the Berlin Wall, a symbol of the cold war, would be torn down. The 1980s in American baseball saw the debuts of three excellent pitchers of Asian Pacific heritage, two of whom would be All-Stars, and the other would be one of the game's great relievers for several years.

"Our Game Too"

Atlee Hammaker

Charlton Atlee Hammaker was born January 24, 1958 in Carmel, California.[cix] Hammaker is of Japanese and German descent. Atlee's father was in the United States Army, so the family moved around quite a bit as he was growing up. He attended high school in Virginia and played baseball, basketball, and football. Hammaker attended East Tennessee State University on a basketball scholarship, but also played baseball for the Buccaneers. He pitched one no hitter in college and had an impressive sixteen wins and four loss record.[cx] Hammaker, a left-handed pitcher, was the twenty-first overall pick by the Kansas City Royals in the 1979 draft, and he made his major league debut in 1981. Hammaker is the only player from ETSU athletics history to be drafted by a MLB team in the first round. During his major league career, Hammaker played for the Kansas City Royals (one year), San Francisco Giants (eight years), San Diego Padres (two years), and Chicago White Sox (two years). His former Giants' manager, Al Rosen, noted that Hammaker was one of his favorite players.[cxi]

It was with the San Francisco Giants that Hammaker spent most of his career. He was traded from the Royals to the Giants in 1982 in a deal involving former all-star and 1971 Cy Young winner, Vida Blue. The 1983 season with the Giants arguably turned out to be Hammaker's best year. He started twenty-three games with a win-loss record of 10-9. He also led the National League with a career low ERA of 2.25. On April 17, 1983, Hammaker came close to pitching a perfect game. The Cincinnati Reds' Johnny Bench broke up the perfect game bid with a single in the eighth inning after Hammaker had retired the twenty-one batters before Bench. The game ended with Hammaker pitching a two-hit shutout as the Giants won 3-0 over the Reds. He followed this game by pitching hitless five innings against the Cubs[cxii].

During this 1983 season, Hammaker made the National League All-Star Game Roster as the starting pitcher. Before the All-Star Game, Hammaker's ERA was 1.70, but shoulder tendinitis would send him to the disabled list in the second half of the season[cxiii]. Hammaker pitched two-thirds of an inning in the All-Star Game at Comiskey Park in Chicago. He gave up seven runs in that inning, including the first All-Star game grand slam to the California Angels' Fred Lynn[cxiv]. Despite the results, Hammaker stated, "Despite what happened, I'd like to go back to the All-Star Game again." [cxv] Hammaker ended up leading the National League in Earned Run Average in 1983 with an ERA of 2.25. Hammaker's 1984 season was cut short due to more injuries. He had surgery on his rotator cuff and then had bone spurs removed from his elbow.[cxvi] He was able to return for the 1985 season and finished with an ERA of 3.74.

Hammaker made it to the post-season twice during his career. In 1987, the Giants battled the St. Louis Cardinals for the NLCS. The Giants fell to the Cardinals in the seven game series. Hammaker pitched eight innings in two games during the series, with an ERA of 7.88. In 1989, the Giants earned the National League Championship by defeating the Chicago Cubs four to one in the series. They fell short of a World Series Championship as the Oakland Athletics swept the series. Atlee pitched as a reliever in two games of the World Series.[cxvii]

He ended his major league career in 1995 with the Chicago White Sox. His total win-loss record was 59-67, and his ERA for his career was 3.66. His total win-loss percentage was .468 over his career. For 1982 and 1983, he was named the MLB's pitcher with best control.[cxviii] Hammaker described his own career as "a rewarding experience," despite injuries that kept him off the mound.[cxix] Hammaker has also noted: "You can't always control results, playing and a lot of other things, but the things that you are in control of, you need to realize that you're trying to glorify God through your actions, speech and attitude."[cxx]

After retirement, Hammaker focused on his family, including five daughters. A near drowning incident with his daughter Christa impacted Hammaker's decision to retire in 1995.[cxxi] Daughter Alesa shared that seeing her father choose family over the sport he loved helped her understand priorities.[cxxii] The MLB is still a part of Hammaker's life, as a new member of his family is currently playing for the MLB. In 2012, his daughter Jenna married MLB player Yan Gomes, who is the first Brazilian-born player to ever play Major League Baseball.[cxxiii] Hammaker has also worked as a pitching instructor at a private baseball facility in the Knoxville, Tennessee area.[cxxiv]

"Our Game Too"

Atlee Hammaker

(Photo Courtesy of Bryan Kuhn Photo Archives)

"Our Game Too"

Atlee Hammaker

(Photo Courtesy of Bryan Kuhn Photo Archives)

Ronald Maurice Darling was born August 19, 1960 in Honolulu, HI and grew up in New England. [cxxv] His mother was of Hawaiian-Chinese descent, and his father was French-Canadian. He attended Yale University, where he was not only a solid pitcher but also a key hitter in the Bulldogs lineup. In 1981, Darling was the starting pitcher against another future Major League hurler, Frank Viola of St. John's, in what many baseball historians acknowledge as the greatest college baseball game ever. While St. John's won that game 1-0 in twelve innings, Darling struck out sixteen batters and threw an unbelievable eleven innings of no-hit baseball.

Ron was drafted by the Texas Rangers organization in the first round of the 1981 amateur draft. Darling was assigned to the Rangers AA team in Tulsa in 1981 and was traded to New York after the season. He spent 1982 and part of 1983 with the Mets AAA team in Tidewater before being called up for his MLB debut on September 6, 1983 against the Philadelphia Phillies, a game he lost 2-0 despite a solid pitching performance. Darling spent the entire 1984 season with the big-league team, earning a spot in the rotation and going 12-9. During his career, he played for the New York Mets (nine years), Montreal Expos (one year), and Oakland Athletics (five years).

"Our Game Too"

Ron Darling

(Photo Courtesy of Bryan Kuhn Photo Archives)

The 1985 season with the New York Mets could be considered Darling's best year in Major League Baseball. That year, he was selected as a National League All-Star and had his career best win-loss percentage of .727, with sixteen wins and six losses. His ERA that year was 2.90, and he pitched a career high 248 innings.[cxxvi] He did, however, also lead the league in walks during the 1985 season with 114.[cxxvii]

While 1985 would be Darling's only All-Star season, his most successful and exciting season from a Mets fan's perspective was the 1986 season. Darling had a win-loss record of 15-6 (.714%), an ERA of 2.81 while throwing four complete games and two shutouts. He also improved his control significantly, decreasing his number of walks from 114 to 81 for the season. In the 1986 National League Championship Series, the Mets defeated the Houston Astros 4-2. Darling pitched five innings in the series, appearing in one game. His ERA was 7.20. The Mets advanced to the 1986 World Series, playing the Boston Red Sox.

The 1986 World Series was an exciting seven game contest between the Mets and Boston Red Sox. The Red Sox had been looking to finally break the "Curse of the Bambino," having not won the World Series since 1918. The Mets defeated the Red Sox four games to three, a heartbreaking loss for many Boston fans. Darling pitched 17.2 innings and appeared in three games during the series (starting games one, four, and seven). He had an earned run average of 1.53 for the World Series.[cxxviii] This series was the best postseason performance of Darling's career. Darling reflected on the series in his 2016 book (with Daniel Paisner), *Game 7, 1986: Failure and Triumph in the Biggest Game of My Life.* When asked what came to mind when his team won the World Series, Darling replied: "My parents...both of my parents taught me how to play. I would have never been there without them. As soon as it was done, all I wanted to see was their faces and their joy. That meant more to me than anything."[cxxix] Darling went on to have several more very good seasons, including going 17-9 in 1988 for the Mets, with seven complete games, four shutouts, and a 3.25 ERA. In 1991, as the Mets were going through a rebuilding phase of sorts, Darling was dealt to the Oakland Athletics. He pitched for the A's, almost exclusively as a starter, until he retired after the 1995 season.

Darling ended his MLB career in 1995, after thirteen years. He won a total of 136 games and lost 116. His Win Loss percentage was .540. His career ERA was 3.87, with a total of thirteen shutouts. He pitched a total of 2360.1 innings during his career.[cxxx] While he was nominated for both National League Rookie of the Year and a National League Cy Young award during his career, Darling placed fifth in both categories. In 1989, however, Ron Darling won the National League Gold Glove in the pitcher category. He was the first pitcher in New York Mets history to win a Gold Glove. Furthering his reputation as a solid hitter, he also hit two homeruns the 1989 season, which were the only homeruns of his MLB career.

Since retirement, Darling has remained connected to baseball with much success. A beloved figure in New York and respected around the MLB, Darling has published two books on baseball: *The Complete Game: Reflections on Baseball and the Art of Pitching*, March 2010 and *Game 7, 1986: Failure and Triumph in the Biggest Game of My Life*, April 2016 (both with Daniel Paisner). Darling made it to number seven on the New York Times Best Sellers list.[cxxxi] He is also an Emmy award winning baseball commentator for the MLB network, TBS, SNY, and WPIX-TV.

"Our Game Too"

Mike Fetters

Michael Lee Fetters, who is of Samoan and Irish ancestry, was born December 17, 1964 in Van Nuys, California but raised primarily in Hawaii. Fetters played baseball at Iolani High School in Honolulu, where he was All-State in both baseball and basketball. Fetters helped his high school win the state championships in both of those sports.[cxxxii] His success on the diamond led to being drafted by the Los Angeles Dodgers in 1983, but Fetters instead chose to accept a scholarship to play college baseball at Pepperdine University in Malibu, CA. Fetters would be drafted again, this time by the California Angels in the 1986 June Amateur Draft. He was the twenty-seventh overall pick. Fetters made his rookie debut in MLB for the Angels on September 1, 1989. During his sixteen-year career, he played for the California (Anaheim) Angels, Milwaukee Brewers, Arizona Diamondbacks, Oakland Athletics, Baltimore Orioles, Los Angeles Dodgers, Pittsburgh Pirates, and Minnesota Twins.

(Photo Courtesy of Bryan Kuhn Photo Archives)

Fetters was one of the top relievers in the game in the mid-1990s, which included the 1996 season in which he saved thirty-two games for the Brewers. Fetters made it to one post-season series with the Arizona Diamondbacks, the 2002 NLDS against the St. Louis Cardinals. He pitched in one inning and had one walk, one strikeout, and gave up one hit. [cxxxiv] The Cardinals won the series 3-0. Fetters was famous in baseball for his pitching motion, particularly his head movement, which he says was a way to relieve stress. In one Bleacher Report article, Fetters' "Mound Stare" was ranked in the top twenty mound stares of all time. Fetters motion has been described as a sudden head movement accompanied by a scowl. Mike Fetters last MLB appearance was in 2004 with the Diamondbacks. He finished his career with 100 saves and was inducted into the Milwaukee Brewers Hall of Fame in 2004. Fetters later said, "I'm proud and humbled by what I've been able to achieve; I don't need to broadcast it. It's one thing I learned living in Hawaii, and I think Marcus Mariota spoke to the heart of it, too: Polynesian people are very humble. Our actions speak for themselves." He is also quoted as saying: "You don't play a sport to become a member of a Hall of Fame — you play because you love the sport, and I do."

After retiring in 2004, Fetters remained connected to baseball, particularly with the Diamondbacks organization. He has broadcasted on radio and TV, and served as a member of baseball operations for the team. [cxxxvii] Fetters currently works with Arizona as a bullpen coach. Prior to this position, he served as an advisor to baseball operations and as a quality control coach. [cxxxviii]

Summary

Coming from various parts of the nation, Hammaker, Darling, and Fetters all made their debut in pro baseball in the 1980s. They would become three of the top pitchers in baseball at various points in their lengthy careers. While each pitcher was able to help their team to the post-season at least once, only Darling would be able to claim a World Series championship. All three pitchers remained involved in baseball after retirement, either in a broadcasting, in the front office, or by working to help kids develop as players. This speaks to their love of baseball and their desire stay connected to the game, a trait shown by baseball players throughout generations, perhaps more so than in any other sport. Baseball is about connections to both the past and future, and the success experienced by Hammaker, Darling, and Fetters would continue to help pave the way for other Asian Pacific American players in future years.

Pitching Statistics for the 1980s

Player	WL %	ERA	Saves	Wins	Losses	Strikeouts	Walks	Innings Pitched
Fetters, Mike	0.431	3.86	100	31	41	518	351	716.2
Darling, Ron	0.54	3.87	0	136	116	1590	906	2360.1
Hammaker, Atlee	0.468	3.66	5	59	67	615	287	1078.2

Chapter Eight

The 1990s

Introduction

The 1990s were a decade of prosperity for many Americans, with an extended economic boom. In 1991, the United States entered the Persian Gulf War, a conflict that still affects our country today although the war has long since ended. Apartheid ended in South Africa after decades, and in China and Eastern Europe, people began to demand more individual freedoms. The 1990s also saw the emergence of mobile phones and cellular technology in American culture. In baseball, scandals and lockouts impacted the national pastime in the 1990s. A strike in 1994 led to the cancellation of the World Series, while salaries and money increasingly became a factor in on-the-field competitiveness. The 1990s brought interleague play to the National and American Leagues and an epic chase to break Roger Maris' single season home run record that would ultimately lead to the exposure of a significant steroid problem in professional baseball. Also, Cal Ripken would break Lou Gehrig's "iron man" record for most consecutive games played. Asian Pacific-American baseball players continued to make an impact on the sport at the end of the twentieth century. This chapter includes profiles of Benny Agbayani, Danny Graves, Johnny Damon, Dave Roberts, Don Wakamatsu, and Onan Masaoka.

Benny Agbayani

Benny Peter Agbayani was born December 28, 1971 in Honolulu, Hawaii. His parents were of Filipino and Samoan descent. He grew up in a tight-knit family, which included his extended family. Many of his relatives lived together under one roof. [cxxxix] Benny started playing Little League baseball when he was just seven years old, and later attended St. Louis High School in Honolulu, where he played baseball, football, and soccer. St. Louis High School is the same high school that was attended by Hank Oana, another Hawaiian born baseball player who made his MLB debut in 1934. [cxl] Agbayani went on to play baseball at Hawaii Pacific University after first going to Oregon Tech to play football. [cxli] He was drafted by the New York Mets in 1993 and assigned to the Mets single-A team in Pittsfield. Agbayani would not make his MLB debut until June 17, 1998. During his career, he played for the New York Mets (four years), Colorado Rockies (one year), and the Boston Red Sox (one year). [cxlii]

Benny was an outfielder during his MLB career and played two post-season series with the Mets. Arguably, Agbayani's most famous hit came in the 2000 NLDS game three against the Giants. After going zero for six in the series, Agbayani hit a walk off home run in the thirteenth inning of game three, sending the Mets on to game four. [cxliii] They won the series, and then beat the Cardinals in the NLCS to advance to the World Series against the New York Yankees. Ultimately, the Yankees won the "subway series." Benny's best Major League season at the plate was 2000 for the Mets, in which he hit fifteen home runs, drove in sixty runs, and had a batting average of .289 while playing 119 games. His final season in MLB was 2002 with the Colorado Rockies and the Red Sox. [cxliv]

After leaving the MLB, Agbayani played six successful seasons in Japan and was a fan favorite. In Japan's Pacific League, he hit 90 homers, had 360 RBIs, and kept a .283 average in 660 games. [cxlv] Since retirement, Agbayani returned to his native Hawaii and worked as an educational assistant in a local high school. [cxlvi] He also continues to coach his kids and participate in local baseball clinics in Hawaii. Additionally, he started a foundation called MYTH: Motivate Yourself to the Highest. [cxlvii]

Benny Agbayani

(Photo Courtesy of Bryan Kuhn Photo Archives)

"Our Game Too"

Danny Graves

Daniel Peter Graves, also known as the "baby faced assassin" was born August 7, 1973 in Saigon, Vietnam. He is the only player in MLB history to have been born in Vietnam. Graves' mother was Vietnamese, and his father was a United States Army Sargent. Graves and his family moved to the United States when he was still a baby, and he went on to play baseball at Brandon High School (Brandon, FL.), and at the University of Miami. [cxlviii] Graves was later inducted into the University of Miami Sports Hall of Fame for his stellar college baseball career as a relief pitcher. [cxlix] Graves was drafted by the Cleveland Indians in the fourth round of the 1994 MLB June Amateur Draft, and began his professional career in the Indians minor league system in 1995 after tearing his ACL in the College World Series. He made his MLB debut on July 13, 1996 for the Indians and would go 2-0 in fifteen appearances for Cleveland that season. [cl] He pitched for the Cleveland Indians, Cincinnati Reds, and New York Mets during his career.

Graves was traded to Cincinnati in 1997, and his most impressive seasons came while in a Reds uniform. For most of his career with the Reds, Graves was used as a relief pitcher, primarily as the team's closer. Graves had multiple seasons with the Reds with over thirty saves, including a career high forty-one saves in the 2004 season. Graves was a two-time National League All-Star, representing the Cincinnati Reds in 2000 and 2004. In 2000, Graves earned the Reds' Ernie Lombardi award (as the team's most valuable player) and the Reds' Johnny Vander Meer Award (as the team's best pitcher). In 2003, Cincinnati unsuccessfully tried to convert him to a starting pitcher, and while he did pitch one shutout and two complete games, his overall record that season was 4-15 in twenty-six starts. [cli] In

2005, in response to a racial slur shouted by a fan as he was leaving the mound, Graves used an obscene hand gesture toward to the fan and was shortly released from the Reds, an unpopular move among his teammates and many Cincinnati fans. He was picked up by the New York Mets for the remainder of the 2005 season and played his final game in the MLB May 9, 2006 as a member of the Cleveland Indians. Danny played minor league baseball through 2008. Graves finished his remarkable MLB career with 182 saves (all with Cincinnati), and is the Cincinnati Reds All-Time career saves leader. As a hitter, Graves had eight MLB career hits, two of which were home runs with the Reds.[clii]

In 2006, Graves returned to Vietnam with his mother, for the first time since they left before Saigon fell during the Vietnam War.[cliii] Graves worked to teach kids in Vietnam baseball and help raise funds for the Vietnam Veterans Memorial fund. He also helped dedicate a baseball field at a local high school where baseball would be taught as part of physical education. Graves has also worked as a baseball analyst, and has appeared on Cincinnati Reds television broadcasts.

"Our Game Too"

Danny Graves

(Photo Courtesy of Bryan Kuhn Photo Archives)

"Our Game Too"

Danny Graves

(Photo Courtesy of Bryan Kuhn Photo Archives)

"Our Game Too"

Johnny Damon

Johnny Damon was born November 5, 1973 in Fort Riley, Kansas. Damon's mother was a Thai immigrant, and his father was a United States Army staff sergeant. Damon attended high school in Orlando and was Baseball America's number one ranked high school baseball prospect in 1992. [cliv] He was drafted after high school as the thirty-fifth overall pick by the Kansas City Royals in 1992, and by 1995 had been called up to the big leagues. Damon, nicknamed the Caveman, made his MLB Debut on August 12, 1995 with the Kansas City Royals. In his first partial season with the Royals, he hit .282 with three home runs, twenty-three RBI, and seven stolen bases in just forty-seven games. By 1996, Damon was an everyday player for the team, splitting time between centerfield and right-field, and remained a fixture in the Royals outfield for the next several years, posting solid offensive numbers. This included leading the American League in stolen bases in 2000. However, he was traded one year before he became eligible for free agency to the Oakland Athletics in January 2001. Damon hit .256 in his one season with Oakland, and then signed as a free agent with the Boston Red Sox prior to the 2002 season. It was with the Boston Red Sox that Damon would become part of one of the most historic teams, and comebacks, in baseball history, which would make him a legend in Red Sox nation.

(Photo Courtesy of Bryan Kuhn Photo Archives)

In 2002, his first season with the Sox, he hit .286 with fourteen home runs, sixty-three RBI, 118 runs, thirty-one steals, and led the league with eleven triples. He followed that up with a solid 2003 season and had a career year in 2004 with 189 hits, twenty home runs, ninety-four RBI, and nineteen steals. But it was the 2004 post-season that defined Damon's career. Damon was a team leader in the clubhouse, and the team had been nicknamed "the idiots" due to their fun-loving, all-out, hard-nosed style of play. The Red Sox rallied from a seemingly hopeless three games to one deficit against their archrival, the New York Yankees, in the ALCS to win the American League Championship, the greatest comeback in MLB postseason history, and advanced to the World Series. In the deciding game seven of the World Series, Damon hit two home runs, including a grand slam. The Red Sox went on to defeat the St. Louis Cardinals in the 2004 World Series, winning their first World Championship since 1918 (eighty-six years) and breaking the infamous "Curse of the Bambino." Damon homered in the World Series as well.

After another very productive season for the Red Sox in 2005 (.316, ten HR, seventy-five RBI, 197 hits), Damon filed for free agency and signed with the New York Yankees prior to the 2006 season. He played four seasons for the Yankees and won a World Series with the team. His final season was 2012 with the Indians. He finished his career with 235 home runs, 1139 RBI, 2769 hits, 1668 runs, and 408 steals. Damon was a two-time All Star with the Boston Red Sox (2002 and 2005) and was nominated for American League MVP four times. [clv] He won two World Series, one with the Boston Red Sox (2004), and one with the New York Yankees (2009). He was also the recipient of the Red Sox Good Guy Award in 2002, and the Red Sox Jensen Spirit Awards in 2004 and 2005. [clvi] During his eighteen years in the MLB, he played for the Kansas City Royals, Boston Red Sox, New York Yankees, Oakland Athletics, Tampa Bay Rays, Detroit Tigers, and Cleveland Indians.

After his career in the MLB, Damon played with the Thailand National Team in the 2013 World Baseball Classic. Since retirement, Damon has appeared on the Animal Planet's Tanked series, NBC's Celebrity Apprentice, and in the major motion picture "Fever Pitch" in 2005, a baseball-themed romantic comedy in which the Red Sox win the 2004 World Series. He also founded the Johnny Damon Foundation, which helps support many charities. [clvii]

"Our Game Too"

Johnny Damon

(Photo Courtesy of Bryan Kuhn Photo Archives)

"Our Game Too"

Dave Roberts

David Day Roberts was born May 31, 1972 in Naha, Okinawa, Japan. Roberts' father was a United States Marine, and his mother was Japanese. He grew up mosqly in the San Diego, California area and was a three-sport athlete in high school, including playing quarterback on the team that won the San Diego Class 3A Championship. [clviii] After turning down college football scholarships, he enrolled at UCLA and earned a spot on the baseball team as a walk-on. [clix] After first being drafted by the Cleveland Indians in the forty-seventh round of the 1993 June draft, he decided to return to school at UCLA. He was later drafted in the twenty-eighth round of the 1994 draft by the Detroit Tigers and was soon assigned to the Tigers single-A team in Jamestown of the New York-Pennsylvania League. Roberts moved through the Tigers minor league system with a respectable batting average while compiling a large number of stolen bases, but was never promoted to Detroit. He was traded in 1998 to the Cleveland Indians organization and eventually made his MLB debut with the Indians on August 7, 1999 as a twenty-seven year old centerfielder. He had three hits and a steal in his first big league game. Roberts was up and down between the big league team in Cleveland at their AA and AAA for several years. However, it would not be until he was traded to the Los Angeles Dodgers before the 2002 season that he would get a chance to play a significant number of games in a major league season.

Roberts played in 127 games with the Dodgers in 2002 with 422 at-bats; this was his first opportunity to prove himself at the big league level. In 2002, the speedy outfielder and frequent leadoff hitter hit .277 with 117 hits, three home runs, thirty-four RBI, seven triples, and forty-five stolen bases. Injuries would somewhat curtail Robert's next couple of seasons in Los Angeles, and he was traded to the Boston Red Sox shortly before the trade deadline in the summer of 2004.[clx] Although Roberts only played part of the 2004 season for the Boston Red Sox, he was part of a legendary Red Sox team and contributed with, perhaps, the biggest stolen base in Boston Red Sox history in the 2004 American League Championship Series vs. the New York Yankees. In that fateful game, the Sox were down 4-3 in the bottom of the ninth inning and would be eliminated from the post-season if they lost this game. Roberts was brought in as a pinch runner at first base for Kevin Millar and stole second base off Yankee closer-extraordinaire Mariano Riviera in an extremely close play. Roberts then scored the tying run from second base on the next hit by Billy Mueller. The Red Sox baseball operations office had acquired Roberts specifically for key moments like the 2004 postseason when pinch-running and speed were needed.[clxi] The Sox went on to win that game in extra-innings and eventually completed the greatest comeback in baseball history by defeating the Yankees four games to three, winning the American League Championship Series and, later, the World Series against St. Louis. This was the Red Sox first World Series since 1918. In forty-five games and 101 plate appearances for the Red Sox that season, Roberts hit .256, with two homeruns, fourteen RBI, and five steals.

After the 2004 season with the Red Sox, Roberts was traded to the Padres. He would put together back-to-back solid seasons for the Padres, including career highs in batting average (.293), Hits (146), Triples (thirteen), and Stolen Bases (forty-nine) in 2006.[clxii] Roberts signed with the San Francisco Giants for 2007 and played that season, and part of 2008, with the team, concluding his MLB career. Roberts ranked fourth in the MLB in stolen bases between 2002 and 2007 and finished his career with a remarkable 243 steals, while being thrown out only fifty-eight times.[clxiii] In his ten years in the MLB, Roberts played for the Cleveland Indians, Los Angeles Dodgers, Boston Red Sox, San Diego Padres, and San Francisco Giants.

Since retiring from playing in the MLB, Roberts survived a battle with cancer at age thirty-seven in 2011, was an analyst for Red Sox games on the New England Sports Network, and worked as a coach and in the front office with the San Diego Padres. He made national headlines when he was hired as the first minority manager in Los Angeles Dodgers history.[clxiv] At the time of his hiring prior to the 2016 season, he was just the third minority manager currently in Major League Baseball. At a news conference regarding his hiring as Dodgers manager, Roberts said, "I am the son of Waymon and Eiko Roberts, and the husband of Tricia Roberts; and I've got two beautiful kids, and I am who I am. I am transparent. I am who I am."[clxv] Roberts was named the 2016 National League Manager of the Year for his success with the Dodgers.

"Our Game Too"
Dave Roberts

(Photos Courtesy of Abby Perry Photo Archives)

Wilbur Wakamatsu

Wilbur Donald Wakamatsu was born February 22, 1963 in Hood River, Oregon. Wakamatsu's mother was Irish-American, and his father was a third generation Japanese-American born in a Japanese American internment camp in California.[clxvi] Don Wakamatsu's family moved from Oregon to Haywood, California when he was young, a place he still considers home. Seattle Times columnist Jerry Brewer said of Wakamatsu, "he never felt different. He turned his multicultural upbringing into an asset, displaying a rare ability to relate to everyone." Besides being a great athlete with professional baseball aspirations, Don had a reputation as the friendliest guy in the room. His parents and grandparents had been a working-class family, and taught Don the value of hard work and humility.[clxvii] He played baseball, football, and basketball at Hayward High School and went on to play baseball at Arizona State, where he earned all-conference honors as a catcher. He was first drafted by the Yankees in the 1984 draft but decided to return to ASU, and was later drafted by the Cincinnati Reds in the eleventh round of the 1985 draft. He began his professional career with the Reds Rookie League team in Billings, Montana of the Pioneer League. He played in the Reds minor league system, advancing as high as double-A through 1988, when the Reds organization released him. The Chicago White Sox picked him up, and after three more minor league seasons, he made his MLB debut May 22, 1991 as a catcher for Chicago. Wakamatsu played in eighteen games for the White Sox, with seven hits, two runs, and a .226 batting average. Those eighteen games for the White Sox in 1991 would be the only big-league games of Wakamatsu's career.[clxviii] He continued to play professionally in the minor league systems of the Dodgers, Rangers, Indians, Mariners, and Brewers through the 1996 season.

After managing in the minor leagues for the Diamondbacks and the Angels, and as a major league coach with the Rangers and the Athletics, he was named the manager of the Seattle Mariners in November 2008, becoming the first Asian-American Manager in Major League Baseball history. Wakamatsu served as the manager for the Seattle Mariners for two years (2009-2010), and finished fourth among the nominees for American League Manager of the Year in 2009. Wakamatsu stated, "If I can set somewhat of a steppingstone for future Japanese-Americans and just the equality in baseball, I'm glad to burden that torch." [clxix] Since his time as manager with the Mariners, Wakamatsu has worked with several other teams. He served as a bench coach for the Toronto Blue Jays, a scout for the New York Yankees, and a bench coach for the 2015 World Series Champion Kansas City Royals. [clxx]

Onan Masaoka

Onan Kainoa Satoshi Masaoka was born October 27, 1977 in Hilo, Hawaii. He is of Japanese ancestry, as well as Chinese, Portuguese, and Hawaiian. His father worked with a local water company, and his mother worked as a school custodian; his family taught him the value of diligence and hard work. [clxxi] He was awarded a scholarship to play college baseball at Miami (FL.), but instead signed with the Los Angeles Dodgers after he was drafted by the team in the third round of the 1995 MLB June Amateur Draft. Masaoka, a powerful left-handed pitcher, would play in the Dodgers minor league system from 1995 through 1998 and made his big league debut on April 5,

1999 with Los Angeles. He pitched in fifty-four games for the Dodgers in 1999, all in relief, going 2-4 with one save. He also spent part of the 2000 season with the team, appearing in twenty-nine games with a 1-1 record. The final major league game of his career would be on September 30, 2000. After playing the first part of the 2001 season with the Dodgers AAA team in Albuquerque, the Dodgers traded Masaoka to the White Sox that summer. Masaoka would play for the White Sox AAA team in Charlotte for the remainder of the season. He attempted a comeback to professional baseball eight years later, appearing in twelve games with the Gary (Indiana) Southshore Railcats, an independent minor league team in the Northern League in 2009.[clxxii] After his professional baseball career, Masaoka retired to Hawaii with his family, played recreational baseball, volunteered as a pitching coach, and earned a business degree from the University of Hawaii.

Summary

This decade saw the presence of Asian Pacific-Americans increase throughout the sport. While there had been outstanding Asian Pacific-American pitchers before who were "high profile," Johnny Damon became the first Asian Pacific-American who was a bonafide superstar as an outfielder. Damon became a baseball icon. The 1990s saw Asian Pacific-Americans in multiple positions on the diamond. Don Wakamatsu becoming the first Asian Pacific-American manager in Major League Baseball was a significant milestone. In many ways, the debut of the players in this decade seemed to make a turning point, and seemed to signal the broader scope of what was to come in the twenty-first century for Asian Pacific Americans in Major League Baseball.

Batting Statistics for Asian Pacific American MLB Players in the 1990s

Player	Runs	Hits	BA	On Base %	RBI	HR	Stolen Bases	Plate Appearances
Agbayani, Benny	145	299	0.274	0.362	156	39	16	1255
Damon, Johnny	1668	276 9	0.284	0.352	113 9	235	408	10917
Roberts, Dave	437	721	0.266	0.342	213	23	243	3092
Wakamatsu, Don	2	7	0.226	0.25	0	0	0	32

Pitching Statistics for Asian Pacific American MLB Players in the 1990s

Player	WL %	ERA	Saves	Wins	Losses	Strikeouts	Walks	Innings Pitched
Graves, Danny	0.494	4.05	182	43	44	429	271	808.1
Masaoka, Onan	0.375	4.23	1	3	5	88	62	93.2

Chapter Nine

The 2000s

Introduction

For many Americans, the defining moment of the 2000s occurred on September 11, 2001 with the terrorist attacks on the United States, a day that would forever change our country and the way we live. Those events took place during the pennant chase of the baseball season, and for many, America's national pastime played a significant role in helping our country to heal. The decade would also bring about the rise of the smartphone in American culture and the first African American President of the United States, Barack Obama. For many, this was symbolic of the changing face of the United States. In baseball, growing speculation about performance enhancing drugs led to congressional hearings and discussions about how to fix the problem, including testing at the major league level. This testing was agreed upon by both the players union and MLB. Giants' slugger Barry Bonds had shattered both the single season home run record and Hank Aaron's career home run record in the wake of speculation about his use of performance enhancing drugs. In 2001, the arrival of Ichiro Suzuki from Japan, who would go on to become the first MLB superstar from Asia, was significant for other players who would come from Asia to play baseball in the United States. Ichiro became one of the best hitters in the game during his career. In 2003, the Boston Red Sox won their first World Series in 86 years, breaking the "Curse of the Bambino." Perhaps more significant than their actual win in the World Series was their come-from-behind series victory against their archrival, the New York Yankees, in the American League Championship

Series. They rallied from a 3-0 deficit for the biggest comeback in baseball post-season history. The Yankees and Sox would be powerful rivals throughout the decade. On the international scene, the World Baseball Classic began in 2006 in an attempt to create interest in the game around the world in a nation vs. nation baseball tournament. Chapter Nine provides a look at Asian Pacific-American baseball players at the start of the twenty-first century. Economically, baseball was very healthy, partially due to large television contracts as well as increased attendance.

According to the U.S. Census Bureau, Asian-Americans were the fastest growing population group in the nation during this decade, growing by forty-six percent from 2000-2010.[clxxiii] These changing demographics could be seen in baseball as well as the 2000s continued to bring a variety of Asian Pacific-American baseball players to national prominence. Profiles in this chapter include Kurt Suzuki, Travis Ishikawa, Brandon League, Billy Sadler, Shane Komine, Charlie Zink, Dane Sardinha, Bronson Sardinha, Shane Victorino, Jeremy Guthrie, Clay Rapada, Geno Espineli, Tim Lincecum, Chris Aguila, Wes Littleton, Matt Tuiasosopo, Brandon Villafuerte, and Jason Bartlett.

Kurt Suzuki

Kurt Kiyoshi Suzuki was born October 4, 1983 in Wailuku, Hawaii. Suzuki is a fourth generation Japanese-American.[clxxiv] He attended Baldwin High School in Wailuku, and then played collegiately at Cal State Fullerton, where he received the Brooks Wallace Award in 2004 as the nation's best college baseball player, as well as the Johnny Bench Award as the nation's best catcher. He had initially come to the university as a walk-on but went on to help Cal State Fullerton win the

College World Series Championship in 2004. [clxxv] Suzuki was drafted in the second round of the 2004 MLB June Amateur Draft by the Oakland Athletics and made his MLB debut June 12, 2007 with the Athletics. In his initial MLB season, Suzuki hit seven home runs and drove in 39 runs with a batting average of .249. He appeared in 68 games. Suzuki would be the A's everyday catcher for the next several years until he was traded to the Washington Nationals in the summer of 2012. After sharing catching duties in Washington, he would be traded back to Oakland in August 2013. After the 2013 season, Suzuki signed as a free agent with the Minnesota Twins and played with the team through 2016, signing as a free agent with the Atlanta Braves for 2017. His best career season came as an Athletic in 2009 when he recorded 156 hits, thirty-seven doubles, fifteen home runs, eighty-eight RBI, eight steals, and a .274 batting average. [clxxvi] In his ten years in the league, he played for the Oakland Athletics, Minnesota Twins, and Washington Nationals.

Suzuki spent his MLB career thus far in the American League playing primarily as catcher. He has also been used as Designated Hitter periodically. In 2014, Suzuki was selected as an American League All Star from the Minnesota Twins. [clxxvii] The Oakland Athletics recognized Suzuki in 2010 and 2011 with the Heart and Hustle Award, and in 2009 with their Jim Catfish Hunter Award. Additionally, in 2013 Suzuki ranked thirteenth in the American League in Batting Average with .288. [clxxviii] In 2016, he became one of the first major league hitters to start using the revolutionary new Axe bat, a bat with a handle similar to an axe. The bat is designed to help hitters produce better power transfer and bat speed. [clxxix] Suzuki went on to hit .258 with eight home runs and forty-nine RBI in just 106 games during the 2016 season. Suzuki and his family are very active in the cities in which he plays, his home state of Hawaii, and California where his family currently lives. He and his wife started a foundation that helps charitable causes, some of which included promoting healthy lifestyles, kidney disease research, and pediatric cancer research. [clxxx]

Travis Ishikawa

Travis Takashi Ishikawa was born September 24, 1983 in Seattle, Washington. Ishikawa is Japanese-American and grew up in the Seattle area. [clxxxi] His grandfather, born in California, was held in an internment camp during World War II, as were thousands of other Japanese-Americans. Ishikawa's father was had been a high school baseball pitcher in California. [clxxxii] The San Francisco Giants drafted Ishikawa in the twenty-first round of the 2002 draft, and he became a top ten Giants prospect. [clxxxiii] He made his MLB debut April 18, 2006 for the San Francisco Giants, and his first Major League appearance came a day later as a pinch hitter. Ishikawa played twelve games with the Giants in 2006 and would not return to the big leagues until 2008. His best career year, statistically, would come in 2009 for the Giants when he appeared in 120 games, had 326 at-bats, eighty-five hits, hit nine home runs, two stolen bases, two triples, and thirty-nine RBI. All of these were career highs. He also hit .261 in 2009. [clxxxiv] Ishikawa is best remembered, however, for a historic at-bat in the post-season for San Francisco.

The famous home run occurred in the bottom of the ninth inning of the fifth game in the NLCS against the St. Louis Cardinals. With a 2-0 count, Ishikawa hit a three run home run in the ninth inning to send the Giants to the World Series. Ishikawa won the "Walk Off of the Year Award." [clxxxv] It was the first walk-off home run to send a National League team to the World Series since the Giants' Bobby Thomson's famous "Shot Heard

"Round The World" in 1951. Ishikawa went on to win two World Series with the San Francisco Giants in 2010 and 2014 and is forever a part of Giants' lore. In all of his post-season series, Ishikawa has been on the winning side every time. In total, he was walked six times in the post-seasons, had a batting average of .271, and an on base percentage of .339.[clxxxvi] In his eight years in the league, he played for the San Francisco Giants, Milwaukee Brewers, Baltimore Orioles, New York Yankees, Pittsburgh Pirates, and was a free agent heading into the 2017 season.[clxxxvii] Throughout his career, the left-handed hitter has played primarily at first base, with some limited playing time in the outfield, and is considered an outstanding defensive first baseman.

Brandon League

Brandon Paul League was born March 16, 1983 in Sacramento, California and played high school baseball in Hawaii. He was selected by the Toronto Blue Jays in the second round of the 2001 draft. League is Japanese=American. The right-handed reliever, known for his hard sinker, made his MLB debut September 21, 2004 for the Toronto Blue Jays. In his eleven years in the league, League played for the Toronto Blue Jays, Seattle Mariners, and Los Angeles Dodgers.[clxxxviii]

The 2011 season was, arguably, League's best in the MLB. League was selected as an American League All Star from the Seattle Mariners. Also in 2011, League was third in the American League with thirty-seven saves for the season, and had an impressive 2.279 earned run average. He had an 88.1% save percentage that year, with only five blown saves. He also had a fifteen save season in 2012, split between the Mariners and the Dodgers, and a fourteen save season with the Dodgers in 2013. League did not play professional baseball in 2016, but signed a minor league contract with the Kansas City Royals in early 2017. [clxxxix]

Billy Sadler

William Henry Sadler was born September 21, 1981 in Pensacola, Florida. Sadler is of partial Japanese descent and played college baseball at Pensacola State and Louisiana State University. The right-handed reliever signed with the San Francisco Giants after being drafted by the team in 2003 and made his MLB debut September 15, 2006 with the Giants. In his three years in the MLB, Sadler appeared in thirty-eight games for the San Francisco Giants and one game for the Houston Astros. His career was cut short by injuries, and after his MLB days were over, he began participating in youth baseball instruction, coaching, and development in the Pensacola area. [cxc]

Shane Komine

Shane Kenji Komine was born October 18, 1980 in Honolulu, Hawaii and played baseball at Kalani High School. Komine is Japanese-American. He played college baseball at the University of Nebraska, where he was an All-American pitcher, and was nicknamed "Hawaiian Punch-Out" by Baseball America. [cxci] The right-hander made his MLB debut on July 30, 2006 for the Oakland Athletics and played the 2006 and 2007 seasons for the team before retiring from the MLB. He appeared in four MLB games in his career, two as a starter. In his final game, Komine pitched in the eighth inning while Kurt Suzuki was the catcher. This was the first battery in MLB history with two players born in Hawaii with Japanese ancestry. [cxcii]

"Our Game Too"

Charlie Zink

Charles Tadao Zink was born August 26, 1979 in Carmichael, California. Zink, son of prison guards at the famous Folsom Prison, is Japanese-American.[cxciii] Zink played college baseball at Savannah (Ga.) College of Arts and Design (a division III school). In fact Red Sox legend Louis Tiant had coached Zink in college and later recommended him to the Red Sox organization. After a tryout, the Sox signed him for the spring of 2002 and designated him to their single A farm team. Zink was a conventional...fastball, curve, changeup...pitcher, but everything changed for him later in 2002 when he was jokingly throwing knuckleballs while playing catch with a coach. Zink had never used the knuckleball before. By 2003, he had become an almost exclusively knuckleball pitcher. This change became a very successful one for Zink, and this success helped him move up through the Sox farm system and get recognized as a legitimate, big-time major league prospect. He drew comparisons to the greatest knuckleball pitchers of all-time. After some ups and down in the minor leagues, which is not unusual for a pitcher throwing the quirky and wonderfully maddening knuckleball, he went 14-6, with a 2.84 ERA and 106 strikeouts for the Red Sox AAA team in Pawtucket, and was named International League (AAA) Pitcher of the Year.[cxciv]

The big league team in Boston took notice, and Zink made his MLB debut on August 12, 2008 for the Red Sox.[cxcv] Zink got the start, and in what would be his only major league game, Zink threw 4.1 innings, giving up eleven hits and eight earned runs, and received a no decision (although the Red Sox went on to win the game). He was sent back to minor leagues after that game at Fenway Park and retired from professional baseball in 2011.[cxcvi] He had played only one major league game, but it was for the Red Sox at Fenway Park. After baseball, Charlie and his family moved to the northern California area.

Dane and Bronson Sardinha

While baseball may not be the number one sport in Hawaii, it was the sport of choice in the Sardinha household. Dane Kealoha Sardinha was born April 8, 1979 in Honolulu, Hawaii. He made his MLB debut September 6, 2003 with the Cincinnati Reds. In his six years in the MLB, Sardinha played for the Cincinnati Reds, Detroit Tigers, and Philadelphia Phillies.

Dane Sardinha's brothers, Duke and Bronson, were also professional baseball players. Duke Sardinha played seven years in the minor leagues, while Bronson Sardinha made it to the MLB. [cxcvii]

Bronson Kiheimahanaomauiakeo Sardinha was born April 6, 1983 in Honolulu, Hawaii. He made his MLB debut on September 15, 2007 with the New York Yankees. He played in one ALDS playoff game with the Yankees, replacing Johnny Damon in the outfield. [cxcviii] The three Sardinha brothers actually got to play one game together during an American Legion youth game, with the brothers playing second base, third base, and shortstop. [cxcix]

"Our Game Too"

Dane and Bronson Sardinha

(Photo Courtesy of Joe Santry)

"Our Game Too"

Bronson Sardinha

(Photo Courtesy of Joe Santry)

"Our Game Too"

Bronson Sardinha

(Photo Courtesy of Joe Santry)

"Our Game Too"

Shane Victorino

Shane Patrick Victorino, known as the "Flyin' Hawaiian (aka "The Big Slippery Fish"), was born November 30, 1980 in Wailuku, Hawaii. Victorino describes his heritage as Portuguese, Hawaiian, Chinese, and Japanese. [cc] He played high school baseball at St. Anthony High School in Wailuku, where he was also a Hawaii track and field state champion. He was drafted by the Los Angeles Dodgers in the sixth round of the 1999 June Amateur Draft and began his professional career with the Dodgers' rookie league team in Great Falls that same year. After spending several years in the Dodgers farm system, the Padres selected him in the Rule 5 draft of 2002. He made his MLB debut April 2, 2003 with the San Diego Padres. Victorino was again selected in the Rule 5 draft, this time by the Phillies in 2004. It was with Philadelphia that he received his first significant playing time, becoming a starting outfielder with the team from 2006 until he was traded to the Dodgers mid-summer of 2012.

After the 2012 season, Victorino signed as a free agent with Boston, becoming the team's starting right fielder for most of the season. Victorino battled injuries for the next two seasons with the Red Sox and was traded to the Dodgers in July 2015. [cci] The Cubs released Victorino in 2016, but he was considering a comeback attempt in 2017. [ccii] In his twelve years in the league, Victorino played for the San Diego Padres, Philadelphia Phillies, Los Angeles Dodgers, Boston Red Sox, and Los Angeles Angels of Anaheim. [cciii] Outside of baseball, he appeared on the hit television series "Hawaii Five-0" in 2012. [cciv]

"Our Game Too"

Shane Victorino

(Photo Courtesy of the Boston Red Sox)

Victorino, in addition to two World Series championships (one with the Phillies in 2008, and one with the Red Sox in 2013), has earned several accolades in the MLB. He earned the 2008 Lou Gehrig award for character and integrity, 2010 Phillies Good Guy Award, and the 2011 Branch Rickey Award for outstanding community service. Victorino was also a two time National League All-Star with the Philadelphia Phillies in 2009 and 2011. He earned three Rawlings National League Gold Gloves with the Philadelphia Phillies in 2008, 2009, and 2010, and also earned a Rawlings American League Gold Glove with the Boston Red Sox in 2013, all as an outfielder. Victorino was also on several leaderboards during his career. He ranked third in stolen bases in 2010 with thirty-four, and fourth in stolen bases in 2012 with thirty-nine. In 2009, his 102 runs scored ranked him seventh in the National League, and he was also ranked seventh again in 2011 with ninety-five. [ccv]

Jeremy Guthrie

Jeremy Guthrie was born April 8, 1979 in Roseburg, Oregon. Guthrie identifies himself as Japanese-American. [ccvi] Guthrie says, "I feel a strong tie with Japanese culture, but I don't know why. I feel close to Japanese players". [ccvii] He played baseball at Brigham Young University his freshman year, and then spent two years as a Mormon missionary in Europe. When he returned to the United States, he played the next two years of college baseball at Stanford before being drafted by Cleveland in 2002. Before signing with the Indians in 2002, he had previously been drafted by other MLB teams but was determined to complete his church mission first, reportedly even turning down a one million dollar signing bonus from the New York Mets. [ccviii] At a MLB World Series press conference in 2014, Guthrie reflected, "what I learned as a missionary in those two years away are the foundation for everything that happens to me in my life". [ccix] Guthrie made his MLB debut August 28, 2004 with the Cleveland Indians. In his twelve years in the MLB, he played for the Baltimore Orioles, Kansas City Royals, Colorado Rockies, and Cleveland Indians. [ccx]

His best career year came in 2013 with the Royals, when he had a 15-12 record with three complete games and two shutouts. Guthrie made it to the post-season in 2014 with the Kansas City Royals. The Royals clinched the American League Pennant, defeating the Baltimore Orioles, but lost to the San Francisco Giants in the World Series. Guthrie had an ERA of 4.05 for 13.1 innings pitched in both of the series combined. He gave up zero homeruns and struck out five batters. He started three games in the 2014 post-season, with a no-decision in the ALCS and a 1-1 record in the World Series. [ccxi]

Guthrie has achieved leaderboard status in several categories during his MLB career. He pitched two shutouts in 2013, which ranked him third among American League pitchers that season. In his career as a whole, Guthrie pitched eight complete games. In 2013, he pitched three of those complete games, which earned him a top place among American League pitchers. In 2009 and 2013, he started thirty-three games each season, which ranked him fourth both years in the American League. Additionally, with fifteen wins in 2013, he ranked sixth overall in the American League. Also in 2013, he ranked first in the American League in hits given up with 236 total. [ccxii]

After leaving the MLB, Guthrie was recruited to play baseball in Australia. [ccxiii] Guthrie was selected by the Jet Couriers Melbourne Aces. In February 2017, Jeremy Guthrie signed a minor league contract with the Washington Nationals, receiving an invitation to spring training. [ccxiv] He and his family make their home in Missouri.

Clay Rapada

Clayton Anthony Rapada was born March 9, 1981 in Portsmouth, Virginia. He played college baseball at division II Virginia State, and was signed as an amateur free agent by the Chicago Cubs in 2002. A Filipino-American, Rapada made his MLB debut on June 14, 2007 with the Cubs. [ccxv] The left-handed pitcher played seven years in the MLB. He pitched for the Chicago Cubs, Detroit Tigers, Texas Rangers, Baltimore Orioles, New York Yankees, and Cleveland Indians. [ccxvi]

Rapada's win-loss percentage of 1.00 is an impressive statistic for his career. Rapada pitched in the most MLB games, a total of 152, without being charged with a loss. In fact, Rapada's 152 games pitched without a loss are the most since 1916 in MLB history. [ccxvii] Additionally, in 2012, Rapada ranked fifteenth in the American League in the category of Games Played with a total of seventy games. [ccxviii]

Because of his Fillipino-American heritage, Rapada was eligible to compete for the Phillipines in the World Baseball Classic, which he did in the qualifying in 2017. In 2016, Rapada began his coaching career when he was hired as the pitching coach for the Augusta Greenjackets, the San Francisco Giants single-A team in the South Atlantic League. [ccxix]

"Our Game Too"

Clay Rapada

(Photo Courtesy of Joe Santry)

"Our Game Too"

Clay Rapada

(Photo Courtesy of Joe Santry)

"Our Game Too"

Clay Rapada

(Photo Courtesy of Joe Santry)

"Our Game Too"

Clay Rapada

(Photo Courtesy of Joe Santry)

"Our Game Too"

Geno Espineli

Eugene MacAlalag Espineli (Geno) was born September 8, 1982 in Houston, Texas. Espineli, born to Filipino immigrants, grew up in Katy, Texas. [ccxx] He was drafted in the fourteenth round of the 2004 June Amateur draft out of Texas Christian University by the San Francisco Giants. He had also previously played baseball for the University of Texas. Espineli made his MLB debut July 16, 2004 with the San Francisco Giants. The left-hander pitched one season for the San Francisco Giants. [ccxxi] While pitching in the Giants minor league system in 2008 for the Fresno Grizzlies, Espineli was named to the Pacific Coast League (AAA) All-Star team. [ccxxii] Espinelli was selected for the United States Olympic Baseball team in 2008 but was not able to play because he was on the big league roster for the Giants at that time. [ccxxiii] He was invited to play on the Phillipines' World Baseball Classic team in WBC qualifying tournament in 2012. [ccxxiv]

Tim Lincecum

Timothy LeRoy Lincecum was born June 15, 1984 in Bellevue, Washington. Lincecum is Filipino-American. [ccxxv] His mother was the daughter of Filipino immigrants. His father helped nurture his love for baseball at a young age. Lincecum played college baseball at the University of Washington and was drafted twice before the Giants selected him in the first round (tenth overall) of the 2006 June Draft. [ccxxvi] While at Washington, he won the 2006 Golden Spikes Award as the nation's best amateur player. Lincecum, nicknamed "The Freak," made a quick transition from college baseball to the big leagues, making his MLB debut on May 6, 2007 for the San Francisco Giants. Through the 2016 season, Lincecum has pitched for ten years in the MLB for the San Francisco Giants and Los Angeles Angels of Anaheim. [ccxxvii]

Lincecum's All-Star career has earned him many accolades. Lincecum was a National League All-Star for four years (2008-2011) with the San Francisco Giants. Additionally, Lincecum earned two Cy Young Awards in 2008 and 2009. For a few years, Lincecum was perhaps the most dominant pitcher in all of baseball. In 2010, Lincecum earned the National League Babe Ruth Award for his post-season excellence. [ccxxviii] In addition, he has pitched two no-hitters (2013 and 2014).

Lincecum has also earned his place at the top of the MLB leaderboard in several categories. In 2008 and 2009, Lincecum ranked second in the National League in the ERA category (2.62 and 2.48), and in 2011 he ranked fifth with an ERA of 2.74. He ranked second, fourth, and sixth in National League Wins for 2008, 2009, and 2010, and led the National League in strikeouts per innings pitched for those three years. He also led the league in shutouts in 2009. Lincecum had the highest winning percentage in the National League in 2008 with .784. [ccxxix]

Lincecum won three World Series Championships with the San Francisco Giants in 2010, 2012, and 2014. Lincecum was a starter in 2010 and served as a relief pitcher in 2012 and 2014. [ccxxx] The Tim Lincecum era in Sanfrancisco ended after 2015. It was a successful run that brought the Giants three World Championships, a return to baseball greatness among MLB teams, and forever wove "the Freak" into the fabric of San Francisco. In 2016, he signed as a free agent with the Los Angeles Angels. He appeared in nine games with the Angels, going 2-6.

Through the 2016 season, Lincecum was one of two MLB pitchers to win multiple World Series, multiple Cy Young awards, throw multiple no hitters, and be selected for multiple All Star games (four). Lincecum was designated for assignment by the Angels in August of 2016. Looking forward to the 2017 season, Lincecum hopes to secure a starting position as opposed to pitching as a reliever.[ccxxxi] Regardless of whether he ever pitches again, his heroics and numbers in San Francisco will ensure that he always has an important place in baseball history.

Chris Aguila

Christopher Louis Aguila was born February 23, 1979 in Redwood City, California.[ccxxxii] Aguila's father is Filipino.[ccxxxiii] Aguila made his MLB debut June 28, 2004 with the Florida Marlins. In addition to the Marlins, Aguila played for the New York Mets during his four years in the MLB.[ccxxxiv] Aguila played all of the outfield positions and served as a pinch hitter during his career. His overall batting average was .230 with an on base percentage of .280. Aguila, along with several other former major leaguers, opened the Nevada Baseball Factory in 2016, a state-of-the-art baseball development facility in Reno.[ccxxxv]

Wes Littleton

Wes Avi Littleton was born September 2, 1982 in Hayward, California.[ccxxxvi] Littleton is of Samoan ancestry.[ccxxxvii] He played collegiately at Cal State Fullerton and made his MLB debut on July 4, 2006 with the Texas Rangers. Littleton, a right-handed pitcher known for his side-arm delivery, pitched his three years in the MLB with the Texas Rangers and in the minor leagues with several other organizations.[ccxxxviii]

Matt Tuiasosopo

Matthew P. Tuiasosopo was born May 10, 1986 in Bellevue, Washington. [ccxxxix] Tuiasosopo is of Samoan ancestry. [ccxl] He made his MLB debut September 5, 2008 with the Seattle Mariners. During his five years so far in the MLB, Tuiasosopo has played for the Seattle Mariners, Detroit Tigers, and Atlanta Braves. [ccxli] Between 2013 and 2016, Tuiasosopo played in the minor leagues until the Braves called him back up. He has mostly been used as a utility player, playing the outfield, corner infield, and middle infield. His best big-league season came in 2013 with the Tigers when he hit .244 with seven homeruns and thirty RBI. Going into the 2017 season, Tuiasosopo remains in the Braves organization. [ccxlii]

Brandon Villafuerte

Brandon Paul Villafuerte was born December 17, 1975 in Hilo, Hawaii and is of Filipino descent. He made his MLB debut on May 23, 2000 with the Detroit Tigers. During his five years in the MLB, the right-handed relief pitcher played for the Detroit Tigers, Texas Rangers, San Diego Padres, and Arizona Diamondbacks. [ccxliii] Since retiring, Villafuerte is a senior field technician at Arizona State Schools for the Deaf and Blind. [ccxliv]

Jason Bartlett

Jason Alan Bartlett was born October 30, 1979 in Mountain View, California and played college baseball for the Oklahoma Sooners. He was drafted in the thirteenth round of the 2001 draft by the Padres. While in the minor leagues, he was traded to the Twins organization, and he made his MLB debut August 3, 2004 with Minnesota. [ccxlv] During his ten years in the

MLB, Bartlett played for the Minnesota Twins, Tampa Bay Rays, and San Diego Padres.

Bartlett had several notable moments during his MLB career. He placed eighteenth in the voting for the American League MVP in 2008. Bartlett was selected as an American League All-Star in 2009, which was an impressive year for the right-handed shortstop. He hit fourteen home runs, knocked in sixty-six RBI, and had thirty steals while batting .320 for the Rays. He played in the post-season in 2006 with the Twins. He also made the post-season in both 2008 and 2010 with Tampa Bay. He officially retired in 2014. Bartlett and his family made their home in Florida and California after his baseball career. Jason and his wife opened a fitness facility in Naples, Florida in 2016. [ccxlvi]

Summary

Asian Pacific Americans who entered the big leagues in the 2000s were at the forefront of some baseball's biggest moments. Although profiled in an earlier chapter, Johnny Damon and Dave Roberts were vital parts of the Red Sox curse-breaking championship run in 2003. Tim Lincecum would become one of the most dominant pitchers in the game during his career, winning three World Series, two Cy Young awards, and pitching two no-hitters. These are certainly hall of fame worthy accomplishments, although his career has been affected by injuries as of late. His Giants' teammate Travis Ishikawa provided a post-season homerun feat that hadn't happened since "the shot heard round the world." Shane Victorino was using his speed and defense to win a Gold Glove and to help two different teams win World Series championships. American players of Asian Pacific heritage had become more commonplace in baseball, along with Asians, Latino and Latino-Americans, African Americans, and Caucasians as the game turned the corner into the twenty-first century.

MLB Batting Statistics

Player	Runs	Hits	BA	On Base %	RBI	HR	Stolen Bases	Plate Appearances
Suzuki, Kurt	432	1071	0.256	0.311	519	83	19	4622
Ishikawa, Travis	114	241	0.255	0.321	137	23	3	1050
Sardinha, Dane	16	25	0.166	0.243	15	3	0	171
Sardinha, Bronson	6	3	0.333	0.417	2	0	0	12
Victorino, Shane	731	1274	0.275	0.34	489	108	231	5164
Tuiasosopo, Matt	41	74	0.206	0.288	45	12	0	404
Aguila, Chris	26	53	0.23	0.28	16	3	2	248
Bartlett, Jason	435	849	0.27	0.336	286	31	123	3521

MLB Pitching Statistics

Player	WL %	ERA	Saves	Wins	Losses	Strikeouts	Walks	Innings Pitched
League, Brandon	0.435	3.65	74	27	35	375	185	532
Sadler, Billy	0	4.53	0	0	1	50	30	49.2
Komine, Shane	NA	4.86	0	0	0	2	9	16.2
Lincecum, Tim	0.553	3.74	1	110	89	1736	669	1682
Villafuerte, Brandon	0.125	4.12	3	1	7	77	60	102.7
Littleton, Wes	0.625	3.690	3	5	3	55	37	102.1
Espineli, Geno	1	5.06	0	2	0	8	8	16
Rapada, Clay	1	4.06	0	8	0	82	51	93
Zink, Charlie	NA	16.62	0	0	0	1	1	4.1
Guthrie, Jeremy	0.457	4.37	0	91	108	1046	506	1764.2

Chapter Ten

The 2010s

Introduction

This decade has been a time of change for the game, change that some view as positive progression to make the game more accessible and others view as diminishing the intricacies of what makes baseball so special. While instant replay became part of baseball in 2008, the current expanded replay system began in 2014 and plays an important role in almost every. Baseball was the last of the major American sports to embrace the replay system. The MLB has been looking at other ways to speed up the game, including an expanded strike zone, changing the intentional walk process, keeping hitters in the batter's box, and even a pitch clock. Time will tell how many of these reforms actually happen in MLB and how it will affect the game.

In 2015, Rob Manfred replaced Bud Selig as MLB Commissioner and has brought many new ideas with him. MLB has also stiffened penalties for those who use drugs, including those drugs that are performance enhancing. Baseball's all-time hit king Pete Rose, who was indefinitely banned from baseball in 1989 for allegedly betting on the game, attempted to be reinstated into the game in 2015. While Commissioner Manfred denied the reinstatement, he did leave the door open for the Cincinnati Reds to celebrate Rose's career. The Reds promptly put Rose into the team's illustrious hall of fame, perhaps the most renowned baseball hall of fame and museum outside of Cooperstown.

Perhaps one of the biggest baseball developments of this decade so far happened in the fall of 2016, with the Chicago Cubs winning their first World Series since 1908, an unimaginable 108-year drought! The economics of the game continue to be very healthy as innovative avenues for fan involvement and broadcasting that are tied to technology bring new streams of revenue into the sport. Chapter Ten provides the final profiles of Asian Pacific Americans in the MLB from 2010 to the 2016 season. Profiles include Hank Conger, Rob Refsnyder, Sean Manea, Tommy Pham, Kolten Wong, Jeremy Guthrie, Darwin Barney, Addison Russell, and the Ross brothers.

Hank Conger

Hyun Choi "Hank" Conger was born January 29, 1988 in Federal Way, Washington and played high school baseball in Huntington Beach, California. Conger's mother immigrated to the United States from South Korea.[ccxlvii] Hank was drafted by the Los Angeles Angels in the first round of the 2006 June Amateur Draft. After putting together several very solid seasons in the Angels minor league system, the catcher made his MLB debut September 11, 2010 with Los Angeles. In his seven years thus far in the major leagues, he has played with the Los Angeles Angels of Anaheim, Houston Astros, and Tampa Bay Rays.[ccxlviii]

Prior to entering the MLB, Conger was selected as a player for the 2010 MLB Futures Team (he was named MVP in the Futures game) and was recognized as the 2010 Most Valuable Player for the Pacific Coast League (AAA). Since he started in the MLB, Conger has been recognized for his character among players in the MLB. Conger earned the 2015 Astros Darryl Kile Award.[ccxlix] The award is presented annually to a player on the Houston Astros or St. Louis Cardinals who is deemed by the local

Baseball Writers chapter as "a good teammate, a great friend, a fine father, and a humble man."[ccl] He also hit eleven home runs and drove in thirty-three runs that year for the Astros; both were career highs. During his major league career, Conger has played (defensively) exclusively at catcher, except for one game in 2015 with the Astros. In that game he played leftfield.[ccli] In February 2017, Conger signed a minor-league deal with the Arizona Diamondbacks.[cclii]

Rob Refsnyder

Robert Daniel Refsnyder was born March 26, 1991 in Seoul, South Korea and was adopted at five months old by the Refsnyder family of California.[ccliii] His father, Clint Refsnyder, was a former college basketball player and introduced Robert to sports at an early age. Robert recalls that he and his Dad would often play one-on-one basketball games in their driveway, "those games (with my dad) were some of my fondest memories."[ccliv] Refsnyder grew up in California and played football, baseball, and basketball at Laguna Hills High School (California). He played quarterback for his high school and lead them to a local championship his senior year.[cclv] After high school, he went on to have a very successful college baseball career at the University of Arizona. While at the University of Arizona, Refsnyder primarily played the outfield and helped lead his team to the 2012 College World Series Championship, where he was named the Most Outstanding Player for the NCAA tournament.

(Photos Courtesy of Bryan Kuhn Photo Archives)

"Our Game Too"

Rob Refsnyder

(Photo Courtesy of Bryan Kuhn Photo Archives)

He was drafted by the Yankees in the fifth round of the 2012 draft and quickly made an impression on the Yankees farm system. He played mainly at second base, produced solid offensive numbers, and was ranked as one of the top prospects in the Yankee organization.[cclvi] He made his MLB debut July 11, 2015 for New York, and the following day, he hit his first major league home run over the Green Monster at Fenway Park against the Red Sox. Refsnyder played for big league for parts of the 2015 and 2016 seasons and is an important part of the team's future going forward.[cclvii] Refsnyder has played outfield, first base, second base, and third base for the Yankees, leading to speculation that the team might use the versatile right-handed hitter as a sort of "super utility player," a baseball position that is becoming more and more valuable and important in today's game.[cclviii] Preparing for the 2017 season with the Yankees, Refsnyder is going to work on his swing. He stated, "The position doesn't matter. I'm just going to try to hit home runs."[cclix]

Refsnyder and his family often work with children's charities and are advocates for adoption and for helping others. Refsnyder claims, "I want people to know that it's okay to be different, and I'm going to be as accessible as I can about it. I have never shied away from it, and if kids want to ask me about it, I'll talk about it. I might make a joke, but I'll never hide from being adopted. I am proud of my family, I play for the name Refsnyder". [cclx] He also says, "I have such a passionate love for my parents. They've given me every opportunity in the world, and I feel so blessed." [cclxi] "I don't know if God has blessed me with being the biggest or the fastest or the strongest, but He has blessed me with a burning desire to be better," stated Refsnyder. [cclxii] Refsnyder is known for his integrity and competitiveness, a trait his Dad says he had at a very early age.

Sean Manaea

Sean Anthony Manaea was born February 1, 1992 in Valparaiso, Indiana. [cclxiii] His father is from Samoa. [cclxiv] Manea played for Indiana State University and was drafted by the Kansas City Royals as the thirty-fourth overall pick in the 2013 draft. [cclxv] Manaea had been a top pitching prospect prior to the draft, ranked the thirteenth best pre-draft prospect by MLB.com but dropped in the draft due to injury concerns. [cclxvi] The Royals traded him to Oakland in 2015, and he made his MLB debut on April 29, 2016 with the Athletics. Manaea is a left-handed pitcher who has been nicknamed "Baby Giraffe." [cclxvii]

Tommy Pham

Thomas James Pham was born March 8, 1988 in Las Vegas, Nevada where he also grew up. Tommy Pham is Vietnamese-American. [cclxviii] Pham made his MLB debut

September 9, 2014 for the St. Louis Cardinals, after the team had drafted him in the sixteenth round of the 2006 draft. While playing for the Memphis Redbirds in the Cardinals minor league system, Pham was named Best Defensive Outfielder in the Pacific Coast League (AAA) for 2015. [cclxix]

In his career with the St. Louis Cardinals thus far, Pham has played all of the outfield positions and is a right-handed hitter. He made it to one post-season, hitting a homerun and driving in two RBI in five plate appearances in the 2015 NLDS series against the Chicago Cubs. The St. Louis Cardinals lost the series to the Chicago Cubs. [cclxx]

Darwin Barney

Darwin James Kunane Barney was born November 8, 1985 in Portland, Oregon. Barney describes himself as one-quarter Korean, one-quarter Japanese, and half American-Hawaiian. [cclxxi] Barney won back-to-back College World Series in 2006 and 2007 while playing for Oregon State. He made his MLB debut August 12, 2010 for the Chicago Cubs. In his seven years thus far in the MLB, Barney has played for the Chicago Cubs, Los Angeles Dodgers, and Toronto Blue Jays. [cclxxii]

Barney has made his mark on the MLB early in his promising career. In 2011, Barney placed 7th among all nominees for the National League Rookie of the Year Honor. In 2012, he won the Rawlings National League Gold Glove Award as a second baseman for the Cubs. In 2012 and 2013, Barney won the Wilson Team Defensive Player of the Year for the Chicago Cubs. He was also awarded the MLBPAA Cubs Heart and Hustle Award in 2011 and 2012. [cclxxiii]

Kolten Wong

Kolten Kaha Wong was born October 10, 1990 in Hilo, Hawaii. Wong is of Chinese-American descent and grew up in Hawaii. [cclxxiv] At Kamehameha High School (Kea'au, HI), he played both football and baseball and was named the 2008 State Player of the Year for baseball. He played college baseball at the University of Hawaii. Kolten's father had played baseball at Southern Cal and taught his son the game from an early age. Kolten's dad would have him chop down trees with a machete to improve his stroke and strength, bringing to the mind the great Red Sox Hall of Famer Ted Williams and his comparisons of swinging a baseball bat to swinging an axe. [cclxxv] It didn't take long for others to recognize his potential; while playing at the Cape Cod summer league, one coach noted, "A left-handed hitting second baseman who can run, steal bases, hit at the top of the lineup, but hit with some power, everybody likes guys like that." [cclxxvi] He was named to the Baseball America All-American team in 2011 while at Hawaii. The right-handed throwing, left-handed hitter was drafted by St. Louis in the 2011 draft as the 22nd overall pick. He was the franchise's Minor League Player of the Year for 2013, and on August 16 of that year, made his MLB debut for the St. Louis Cardinals. He has played for the St. Louis Cardinals for all four of his seasons thus far. His breakout season with the Cardinals came in 2015 when he hit .22 with 11 home runs, 61 runs batted in, and 15 steals. [cclxxvii]

Wong has appeared in six post-season series with the Cardinals through 2016. He hit 4 homeruns, had 7 RBIs, and a batting average of .204 with 50 plate appearances in those series. Wong and the Cardinals clinched the National League Pennant in 2013 but lost the World Series to the Boston Red Sox.[cclxxviii] Although Wong's career is just beginning, he has made the leaderboard and earned accolades among MLB players. In 2014, Wong was named the National League Rookie of the Month. Additionally, he came in third place in the National League Rookie of the Year voting for 2014. In 2016, Wong ranked eighth in the National League for triples. [cclxxix]

Addison Russell

Addison Warren Russell was born January 23, 1994 in Pensacola, Florida and is Filipino-American. [cclxxx] Russell was drafted by the Oakland Athletics with the 11th pick of the 2012 draft, and traded to Chicago in the summer of 2014. Russell was ranked as one of the top five prospects in the game by Baseball America in 2015, and he made his MLB debut for the Chicago Cubs on April 21, 2015. [cclxxxi] The right-handed hitting second baseman/shortstop made an immediate impact on the Cubs in 2015 and followed that season up with an outstanding 2016, in which he hit 21 home runs with 95 RBI as the team's starting shortstop.

Although his career has been brief, it will be difficult to top the 2016 season for Russell. His team, the Chicago Cubs, won their first World Series Championship in 108 years. Russell was selected as a National League All Star in the 2016 season and topped several of the MLB leaderboards. He was ranked 11th in Runs Batted In for the National League and was 8th overall in the National League for Hits by a Pitch. [cclxxxii] In the 2016 World Series, the twenty-two year old Russell became the youngest player since 1953 (Mickey Mantle) to hit a grand slam in the fall classic. [cclxxxiii] Even at a young age, Russell's place in baseball history is already secure as a member of the Cubs team that broke the "Curse of the Billy Goat" in 2016. The Chicago Cubs had not won a World Series since 1908, and the "Curse of the Billy Goat" was blamed for the draught in championships. According to legend, the Cubs had a curse placed on them in 1945 when a local tavern owner and his pet goat were not allowed to watch a Cubs game at Wrigley field due to the foul smell of the animal, although it should be noted that the goat had a ticket. The 2016 championship erased the Cubs' curse, and secured the 2016 team and Russell as heroes in the Windy City.

Tyson and Joe Ross

Tyson Ross was born on April 22, 1987 in Oakland, California and is of Korean heritage. [cclxxxiv] His father worked as a pediatrician, and his mother was a nurse. [cclxxxv] Ross played college baseball at the University of California in nearby Berkeley and was drafted by a nearby team, the Oakland A's, in the 2nd round of the 2008 draft. The right-handed pitcher was considered one of the A's top minor league prospects in 2010 and made his MLB debut for the team on April 7, 2010. He played with the A's from 2010 to 2012 before he was traded to the San Diego Padres after the 2012 season. It is with the Padres that Ross has found his greatest success. Ross was a National League All-Star in 2014 with an ERA of 2.81 and led all National League pitchers in starts for 2015 with 33. Ross is also considered a good hitting pitcher, and in 2015 had a .250 batting average with one home run and six RBI. [cclxxxvi] On January 19, 2017, Ross signed as free agent with the Texas Rangers. Before turning pro, Tyson played on the United States Jr. National Baseball team and has represented the USA in the Pan-American games. [cclxxxvii]

Baseball success runs in the family for Tyson Ross. His brother Joe, who is also a pitcher, currently plays for the Washington Nationals. The younger Ross was born on May 21, 1993 in Berkeley and attended the same high school his older brother did, Bishop O/Dowd High School in Oakland. The right-hander was drafted by the San Diego Padres as the twenty-fifth overall pick in the 2011 draft.[cclxxxviii] Joe Ross was traded to the Washington Nationals after the 2014 season and was ranked as a Top 100 prospect by ESPN's Keith Law.[cclxxxix] Ross made his debut for the Nationals against the Cubs on June 6, 2015 as the starting pitcher for Washington. While the Ross brothers have yet to face each other as starting pitchers in the same game in MLB, their teams have played each other. To prepare for the occasion, their mom had a special jersey created, half Nationals and half Padres.[ccxc]

Summary

The current decade has brought many young and exciting new Asian Pacific-American players to MLB rosters. Along with many players who debuted in the previous decade, these Asian Pacific-American players are poised to play an important part in the story of baseball. As the Asian Pacific-American population in the United States continues to grow at unprecedented rates, more and more will no doubt find their way to baseball. This is in addition to the wave of established players who have come to the United States from Japan and Korea recently to play Major League Baseball. Addison Russell and Kolten Wong are young players who likely have not even reached their prime yet and have already won World Series. Rob Refsnyder is poised to become a key player going forward. While the percentage of Asian Pacific-American players still lags behind the Asian Pacific-American population, the numbers seem poised to rise with several other players of Asian Pacific American heritage playing college baseball or working their way through the minor leagues.

Batting Statistics for the 2010 Decade

Player	Runs	Hits	BA	On Base %	RBI	HR	Stolen Bases	Plate Appearances
Conger, Hank	94	224	0.221	0.294	114	31	0	1134
Refsnyder, Rob	28	51	0.262	0.332	17	2	4	222
Pham, Tommy	54	77	0.245	0.333	35	14	4	358
Wong, Kolten	168	330	0.248	0.309	126	28	45	1469
Barney, Darwin	263	547	0.249	0.297	176	25	22	2397
Russell, Addison	127	240	0.24	0.314	149	34	9	1121

Pitching Statistics for the 2010 Decade

Player	WL %	ERA	Saves	Wins	Losses	Strikeouts	Walks	Innings Pitched
Manaea, Sean	0.438	3.86	0	7	9	124	37	144.2
Ross, Tyson	0.376	3.64	1	32	53	633	271	670.2
Ross, Joe	0.545	3.52	0	12	10	162	50	181.2

Chapter Eleven

The Future of Asian Pacific American Baseball

Introduction

In the past hundred years, the game of baseball has faced minimal changes in official rules with only a few exceptions. The diversity of the players, however, has changed. The makeup of teams, managers, coaches, and MLB staff more closely mirror the population of the United States today. This final chapter focuses on current trends of diversity in Major League Baseball, current initiatives, and an exploration of the future for Asian Pacific-Americans in the game.

Diversity in the MLB

For the past eleven years, The Institute for Diversity and Ethics in Sports has published a sport-by-sport analysis of racial and gender composition. *The 2016 Racial and Gender Report Card: Major League Baseball* showed an increase in racially progressive hiring practices in MLB. The league was given a score of 90.5 in racial hiring practices, equating to a grade of an A. [ccxci] The data was collected through March 30, 2016. The Asian category in the report may include players who are actually from Asia, as well as Asian Pacific Americans. According to the Bleacher Report, although the number of Asians in the MLB remains small, there are a "disproportionate number" who are successful in the big leagues. [ccxcii]

The report on leadership in the MLB shows an overall trend toward increased diversity throughout all parts of baseball.

For MLB Central Office Staff, 4.6% were reported as Asian, and that is the highest percentage in the past ten years of data collection. For the Senior Administrators category, Asian was reported at 2.4% for 2015, down slightly from its highest reported figure of 2.9% in 2012. Team Professional Administration was reported as 3.9% in 2015, virtually unchanged from the 4% in 2014. The Vice-President category has remained near the 2015 report of 1.7% in recent years. The highest percentage of Asian Vice-Presidents in MLB was 3.2% in 2004. Both 2015-2016 reported data for the General Manager/Director of Player Personnel reached the highest reported percentage of Asians with 3.3% total. The largest percentage of Asians in the MLB was reported in the Physicians category with 6.7% reported for 2015. [ccxciii]

Some of the data on leadership in MLB, however, did not show an increase of Asian presence. In the category of Majority Owners, for example, the percentage has remained at zero since data collection was first reported in 2006. Asian Managers in the MLB have remained at zero percent since 2011, until the hiring of Dave Roberts as the Dodgers Manager prior to the 2016 season. Similarly, Asian Coaches in the MLB were reported as zero percent for both 2014-2015. The data for Head Trainers also remained at zero percent for 2014-2015. [ccxciv]

Since the category of Asian was added to the report of player diversity in MLB in 2002, the percentage has varied. The overall percentage of players identified as Asian increased from 1.2% in 2015 to 1.7% in 2016. The highest number of reported Asian players was 3.0% in 2005. Again, these percentage includes all players who self-reported Asian heritage, both Asian and Asian Pacific-Americans.

In order to compare these numbers from Major League Baseball to the American population as a whole, data on race-based self-identification from the U.S. Census Bureau were used.[ccxcv] Since 1997, Asian and Native Hawaiian and Other Pacific Islander have been reported as separate categories. In 2014, 20.3 million Americans reported themselves as Asian alone or Asian in combination with another census group. In the same year, 1.5 million Americans reported themselves in the Native Hawaiian and Other Pacific Islander category alone or in combination.[ccxcvi] The U.S. Census Bureau reported that as of July 1, 2015, the percentage of Asians in America was 5.6% and the percentage of Native Hawaiian and Other Pacific Islander was .2%. This means, that the combined percentage of Asian and Native Hawaiian and Other Pacific Islander in the United States was just under 6% total.[ccxcvii]

Diversity Initiatives

The Minor League Baseball Diversity Initiative was established in 2009, and it advocates for diversification in the game as well as in the business of baseball.[ccxcviii] Furthermore, the league offers a "Fostering Inclusion through Education and Leadership Development" (FIELD) program to offer participants a direct pathway to a career in baseball.[ccxcix]

"Our Game Too"

Bronson Sardinha signing autographs as member of the Columbus Clippers, AAA team of the Indians.

(Photo courtesy of Joe Santry)

Major League Baseball has also focused on diversity initiatives on the field as well as in other baseball related roles. Most recently, the 2016 Winter Meetings for Major League Baseball included a special event for MLB club personnel and minor league baseball club personnel on diversity and inclusion. [ccc] Additionally, MLB has focused on Diversity Business Summits as well as the Diverse Business Partners program to increase and develop partnerships with minority and female owned businesses. [ccci]

The first Urban Youth Academy was formed in 2006 in Compton, California. The purpose of the organization is to provide opportunities for youth to play baseball and softball in a safe environment while helping the participants impact their urban communities. In addition, the Urban Youth Academy prepares urban athletes for college and professional baseball. [cccii] The Urban Youth Academy has already reported success from their participants. In 2015, three players from the Compton Urban Youth Academy earned Division I Scholarships to play baseball in college. [ccciii] In addition to the Compton location, there are currently Urban Youth Academies in Puerto Rico, Houston, Philadelphia, New Orleans, and Cincinnati. [ccciv]

Another diversity initiative in MLB is the Reviving Baseball in Inner-Cities (RBI) program. The RBI program began providing baseball and softball opportunities for children aged thirteen to eighteen in 1989. The Junior RBI program, serving children aged five to twelve, was added in 2010. In addition to baseball, the program emphasizes character education based on the values that were demonstrated by baseball hall of famer Jackie Robinson. [cccv]

Beyond encouraging youth in inner cities to play baseball, the program aims to help players achieve their dreams. The RBI program also offers scholarships awarded to assist a dozen former participants attend college each year. Additionally, in the 2015 MLB draft, ten players with connections to the program were drafted. [cccvi]

"Our Game Too"

Hall of Fame

As of the printing of this book, none of the Asian Pacific American baseball players profiled in this book have been inducted into the Baseball Hall of Fame. Perhaps the future will include some of the players profiled in this book being inducted in Cooperstown. Although not an Asian Pacific-American, Ichiro Suzuki is poised to become the first Asian MLB player inducted into the Hall of Fame when he retires. Suzuki, an international icon, recently passed 3,000 career MLB hits. Suzuki has over 4,000 total hits in his professional career in Japan's highest-level league and the MLB combined.

Future

Asian-Americans are the fastest growing segment of the American population and are projected to overtake African Americans by 2065 as the third largest group in the United States. As this growth continues, the presence and impact of Asian-Americans will likely increase in all areas of American life, including sports and, more specifically, baseball. While the current percentage of Asian Pacific-Americans playing the game is at its highest level, it is not yet equal to the group's six percent of the national population. Many Asian Pacific-American players in the major leagues are still in the prime of their career, ensuring that they will play an important part in baseball for a long time. Meanwhile in 2017, minor league prospects of Asian Pacific-American descent, including Ian Kahaloa, Jordan Yamamoto, Joe Ross, Kodi Medeiros, and others, are working their way through MLB farm systems preparing for their shot in MLB. It is the diversity of America that makes this country beautiful, strong, and full of hope. Diversity brings these same attributes to our national pastime. As our country grows and the lines of diversity become blurred, hopefully what unites us will take precedence over whatever difference remains. For many Americans, what unites us, regardless of who we are, is the magical game of baseball, where every man that plays feels like a little boy, and hope is renewed with the next pitch.

Appendices

Appendix A Timeline of Asian Pacific American MLB Players

Appendix B Pitching Statistics for Asian Pacific American MLB Players

Appendix C Batting Statistics for Asian Pacific American MLB Players

"Our Game Too"

Timeline of Asian Pacific American MLB Players

Name	Year	Team
Williams, John	1914	Detroit Tigers
Oana, Henry	1934	Philadelphia Phillies
Balcena, Bobby	1956	Cincinnati Redlegs
Lum, Mike	1967	Atlanta Braves
Solaita, Tony	1968	New York Yankees
Wilcox, Milt	1970	Cincinnati Reds
Kurosaki, Ryan	1975	St. Louis Cardinals
Sakata, Lenn	1977	Milwaukee Brewers
Hammaker, Atlee	1981	Kansas City Royals
Darling, Ron	1983	New York Mets
Fetters, Mike	1989	California Angels
Wakamatsu, Don	1991	Chicago White Sox
Damon, Johnny	1995	Kansas City Royals
Graves, Danny	1996	Cleveland Indians
Agbayani, Benny	1998	New York Mets
Masaoka, Onan	1999	Los Angeles Dodgers
Roberts, Dave	1999	Cleveland Indians
Villafuerte, Brandon	2000	Detroit Tigers
Sardinha, Dane	2003	Cincinnati Reds
Victorino, Shane	2003	San Diego Padres
Aguila, Chris	2004	Florida Marlins
Bartlett, Jason	2004	Minnesota Twins
Guthrie, Jeremy	2004	Cleveland Indians
League, Brandon	2004	Toronto Blue Jays
Ishikawa, Travis	2006	San Francisco Giants
Komine, Shane	2006	Oakland Athletics
Littleton, Wes	2006	Texas Rangers
Sadler, Billy	2006	San Francisco Giants

Lincecum, Tim	2007	San Francisco Giants
Rapada, Clay	2007	Chicago Cubs
Sardinha, Bronson	2007	New York Yankees
Suzuki, Kurt	2007	Oakland Athletics
Espineli, Geno	2008	San Francisco Giants
Tuiasosopo, Matt	2008	Seattle Mariners
Zink, Charlie	2008	Boston Red Sox
Barney, Darwin	2010	Chicago Cubs
Conger, Hank	2010	Los Angeles Angels of Anaheim
Ross, Tyson	2010	Oakland Athletics
Wong, Kolten	2013	St. Louis Cardinals
Pham, Tommy	2014	St. Louis Cardinals
Refsnyder, Rob	2015	New York Yankees
Ross, Joe	2015	Washington Nationals
Russell, Addison	2015	Chicago Cubs
Manaea, Sean	2016	Oakland Athletics

Pitching Statistics for Asian Pacific American MLB Players

Player	WL %	ERA	Saves	Wins	Losses	Strikeouts	Walks	Innings Pitched
Darling, Ron	0.540	3.870	0	136	116	1590	906	2360.1
Espineli, Geno	1.000	5.060	0	2	0	8	8	16
Fetters, Mike	0.431	3.860	100	31	41	518	351	716.2
Graves, Danny	0.494	4.050	182	43	44	429	271	808.1
Guthrie, Jeremy	0.457	4.370	0	91	108	1046	506	1764.2
Hammaker, Atlee	0.468	3.660	5	59	67	615	287	1078.2
Komine, Shane	NA	4.860	0	0	0	2	9	16.2
Kurosaki, Ryan	0.000	7.620	0	0	0	6	7	13
League, Brandon	0.435	3.650	74	27	35	375	185	532
Lincecum, Tim	0.553	3.740	1	110	89	1736	669	1682
Littleton, Wes	0.625	3.690	3	5	3	55	37	102.1
Manaea, Sean	0.438	3.860	0	7	9	124	37	144.2
Masaoka, Onan	0.375	4.230	1	3	5	88	62	93.2
Oana, Henry	0.600	3.770	1	3	2	18	26	45.1
Rapada, Clay	1.000	4.060	0	8	0	82	51	93
Ross, Joe	0.545	3.52	0	12	10	162	50	181.2
Ross, Tyson	0.376	3.64	1	32	53	633	271	670.2
Sadler, Billy	0.000	4.530	0	0	1	50	30	49.2
Villafuerte, Brandon	0.125	4.12	3	1	7	77	60	102.7

Wilcox, Milt	0.513	4.070	6	119	113	1137	770	2016.2
Williams, John	0.000	6.350	0	0	2	4	5	11.1
Zink, Charlie	NA	16.620	0	0	0	1	1	4.1

Batting Statistics for Asian Pacific American MLB Players

Player	Runs	Hits	BA	On Base %	RBI	HR	Stolen Bases	Plate Appearances
Agbayani, Benny	145	299	0.274	0.362	156	39	16	1255
Aguila, Chris	26	53	0.23	0.28	16	3	2	248
Balcena, Bobby	2	0	0	0	0	0	0	2
Barney, Darwin	263	547	0.249	0.297	176	25	22	2397
Bartlett, Jason	435	849	0.27	0.336	286	31	123	3521`
Conger, Hank	94	224	0.221	0.294	114	31	0	1134
Damon, Johnny	1668	2769	0.284	0.352	1139	235	408	10917
Ishikawa, Travis	114	241	0.255	0.321	137	23	3	1050
Lum, Mike	404	877	0.247	0.319	431	90	13	4001
Oana, Henry	8	16	0.308	0.321	10	1	0	53
Pham, Tommy	54	77	0.245	0.333	35	14	4	358
Refsnyder, Rob	28	51	0.262	0.332	17	2	4	222
Roberts, Dave	437	721	0.266	0.342	213	23	243	3092
Russell, Addison	127	240	0.24	0.314	149	34	9	1121
Sakata, Lenn	163	296	0.23	0.286	109	25	30	1423
Sardinha, Bronson	6	3	0.333	0.417	2	0	0	12
Sardinha, Dane	16	25	0.166	0.243	15	3	0	171

Solaita, Tony	164	336	0.255	0.357	203	50	2	1554
Suzuki, Kurt	432	1071	0.256	0.311	519	83	19	4622
Tuiasosopo, Matt	41	74	0.206	0.288	45	12	0	404
Victorino, Shane	731	1274	0.275	0.34	489	108	231	5164
Wakamatsu, Don	2	7	0.226	0.25	0	0	0	32
Wong, Kolten	168	330	0.248	0.309	126	28	45	1469

Endnotes

[i] Bergman, 2011.

[ii] Macur, 2008.

[iii] Reaves, 2002, p. 19-23.

[iv] Bergman, 2011. Four million players play baseball in China as opposed to 300 million people who play basketball.

[v] Reaves, 2002.

[vi] Ibid. p. 14.

[vii] Whiting, Chrysanthemum, p. 38-67; Reaves, 2002, p 7-8.

[viii] Ellsessor, 2007.

[ix] Regalado, 2013.

[x] Regalado, 2013.

[xi] Reaves, p. 140-144.

[xii] Ibid.

[xiii] YMCA Archives, "Philip L. Gillett," 1901

[xiv] Reaves, 2002, p. 105-107.

[xv] Baseball Federation of Asia, accessed 3.17.2016

[xvi] World Baseball Softball Confederation. WBSC.org Mongolia Olympic Committee to boost baseball/softball with eyes on Tokyo 2020 Games February 14, 2017

[xvii] Baseball Federation of Asia. Thailand: History of Thai Baseball. http://www.baseballasia.org/BFA/include/index.php?Page=9-1-N

[xviii] Baseball Federation of Asia: Hong Kong. http://www.baseballasia.org/BFA/include/index.php?Page=9-1-6

[xix] World Series, Little League, accessed 3.17.2016.

[xx] Moratal, 2016.

[xxi] Kruth, Cash. August 3, 2016. Baseball Softball to Return to the Olympics in 2020.

[xxii] World Baseball Classic. http://www.worldbaseballclassic.com/

[xxiii] Lara-Cinisomo, Vince. November 15, 2016. 2017 World Baseball Classic Schedule and Scores.

[xxiv] Olympic Council of Asia, accessed 3.17.2016

[xxv] Staples, 2011.

[xxvi] US Census data, 2016

[xxvii] Baseball-reference.com, John Brodie Williams biographical information. Accessed June 30, 2016.

[xxviii] Dawes, 1968.

[xxix] Barton, www.ImmigrationtoUnitedStates.org Accessed June 30, 2016

[xxx] Bruske, "Detroit Duly Delighted."

[xxxi] Stevenson, 1910.

[xxxii] Costello, "Johnny Williams." www.sabr.org. Accessed June 29, 2016.

[xxxiii] Baseball-reference.com. "Johnny Williams Register Statistics and History." www.bbref.com. Accessed June 29, 2016.

[xxxiv] "American League Notes."

[xxxvxxxv] Stump, 1996.

[xxxvi] Ibid.

[xxxvii] Franks, 2008. 158-160.

[xxxviii] Costello, "Prince Oana." www.sabr.org. Accessed June 29, 2016.

[xxxix] Ardolino, 2002.

[xl] Baseball-reference.com. "Tony Rego." www.bbref.com.

[xli] Sandoval, Jim. "Tony Robello." www.sabr.org. Accessed June 29, 2016.

[xlii] Baseball-reference.com. "Tony Robello." www.bbref.com.

[xliii] Franks, 2008. P. 161.

[xliv] Watson, 1932.

[xlv] Ibid.

[xlvi] Nelson, 2004.

[xlvii] Greene, 1943.

[xlviii] Baseball-reference.com "Prince Oana." www.bbref.com.

[xlix] Kritzer, 1946.

[l] Siegel, 1991.

[li] Lemke, 1991.

[lii] Baseball-reference.com "Prince Oana." www.bbref.com.

[liii] Costello, "Prince Oana." www.sabr.org. Accessed June 29, 2016.

[liv] Lariosa, Joseph. June 26, 2013. Fil-Am was 1st Asian to play in major league baseball.

[lv] Baseball-reference.com Bobby Balcena

[lvi] Hillinger Charles, January 10, 1990. http://articles.latimes.com/1990-01-10/sports/sp-207_1_san-pedro

[lvii] Hillinger, Charles, January 10, 1990. http://articles.latimes.com/1990-01-10/sports/sp-207_1_san-pedro

[lviii] www.baseball-reference.com/bullpen/1960's

[lix] Franks, Joel p. 98.

[lx] National Baseball Hall of Fame. Baseballhall.org/discover/the-first-of-many

[lxi] National Baseball Hall of Fame. Baseballhall.org/discover/the-first-of-many

[lxii] History.com/this-day-in-history/first-japanese-player-makes-mlb-debut/

[lxiii] Baseball-reference.com Masanori Murakami

[lxiv] Ciampaglia, Dante A. Jul 14, 2015. Masanori Murakami: Baseball's Forgotten Pioneer.

[lxv] Associated Press, "51 Homers! Yanks Hope for Samoa the Same," *The Binghamton Press*, March 16, 1969.

[lxvi] Durso, Joseph. "Solaita, Big Hitter from South Pacific, Bids for Starring Role in Yankee Cast," *The New York Times*, September 24, 1968.

[lxvii] Hy Goldberg, "Sports in the News," *The Newark News*, March 3, 1969.

[lxviii] Baseball-reference.com Tony Solaita

[lxix] http://m.mlb.com/player/122523/tony-solaita

[lxx] Miller, Dick. "Samoa's Solaita No. 1 Angel," *The Sporting News*, September 11, 1976.

[lxxi] "Tony Solaita Killed in Tafuna Shooting Saturday," *The Samoa News*, February 12, 1990.

[lxxii] Franks, Joel. P. 172.

[lxxiii] Minshew, Wayne. "Lum Best No. 4 Picket, Says Other Lum," *The Sporting News*, July 5, 1969.

[lxxiv] Keyser, Tom. "The Man Who Hit for Hammerin' Hank," *The Calgary Herald*, March 29, 1998, p. B7

[lxxvlxxv] Baseball-reference.com Mike Lum

[lxxvi] Kaneshiro, Stacy. September 26, 2002. Passing up football was wise decision for Lum.

[lxxvii] Baseball-reference.com Mike Lum

[lxxviii] MLB.com Mike Lum.

[lxxix] BaseballAlmanac.com. 1976 Cincinnati Reds Roster.

[lxxx] Feldmann, Doug. (2009). The 1976 Cincinnati Reds: Last Hurrah for the Big Red Machine. McFarland.

[lxxxi] "Lum Performs Magic on Stage and at Bat," *The Sporting News*, September 26, 1981

[lxxxii] Murray, Todd. August 29, 2015. Coach Lum loving life in Pirates' baseball system.

[lxxxiii] Kaneshiro, Stacy. September 26, 2002. Passing up football was wise decision for Lum.

[lxxxiv] Baseball-reference.com Wendell Kim

[lxxxv] Rains, Sally Tippett. February 15, 2015. Whatever Happened to Wendell Kim? The Sad Story.

[lxxxvi] Baseball-reference.com Wendell Kim

[lxxxvii] Brown, Dave. February 16, 2015. Former Giants, Red Sox and Cubs coach Wendell Kim dies at 64.

[lxxxviii] Kim, Wendell, Rains, Sally Tippett. Youth Baseball: A Coach's and Parent's Guide (The Art & Science of Coaching Series) Paperback – May 1, 1998. Coaches Choice.

[lxxxix] Costello, Rory. Lenn Sakata.

[xc] Baseball-reference.com. Lenn Sakata.

[xci] Ibid.

[xcii] Hayes, Anthony. "All American Pastime," May 25, 2000. www.asianweek.com

[xciii] Baseball-reference.com Lenn Sakata

[xciv] MiLB.com. Sakata returns to San Jose dugout.

[xcv] MLB.com. Lenn Sakata.

[xcvi] Baseball-reference.com Milt Wilcox

[xcvii] Ibid.

[xcviii] Ibid.

[xcix] http://www.baseball-fever.com/showthread.php?9017-Almost-Perfect-Perfect-Games

[c] Sutton, Keith. With Two Out in the Ninth - The Almost No-Hitters.

[ci] MLB.com Milt Wilcox.

[cii] Prewitt, Alex. Ex-Detroit Tiger Milt Wilcox Has Gone to the Dogs.

[ciii] Horn, John. September 15, 2011. Milt Wilcox: From World Champion to Royal Oak Icon.

[civ] Kaneshiro, Stacy. August 15, 2002. Kalani's Sakata, Kurosaki major achievers.

[cv] Baseball-reference.com Ryan Kurosaki

[cvi] Regalado, 2013.

[cvii] Nakagawa, Kerry. Japanese-American Baseball in California: A History

[cviii] Kaneshiro, Stacy. August 15, 2002. Kalani's Sakata, Kurosaki major achievers.

[cix] Baseball-Reference.com, Atlee Hammaker.

[cx] ETSU Hall of Fame Members.

[cxi] Kroner, Steve. April 2005.

[cxii] Baseball-Reference.com

[cxiii] Kroner, Steve. April 2005.

[cxiv] Baseball-Reference.com Atlee Hammaker

[cxv] Barnes, Mike. March 1986. Atlee Hammaker Now Knows It Was a Mistake.

[cxvi] Ibid.

[cxvii] Ibid.

[cxviii] ETSU Hall of Fame Members.

[cxix] Kroner, Steve. April 2005.

[cxx] Stokes, Matthew. March 2012.

[cxxi] Ibid.

[cxxii] Ibid.

[cxxiii] Shulman, Henry. April 2014. For Atlee Hammaker, more ball in the family seemed like bad idea.

[cxxiv] http://www.sfgate.com/sports/article/WHERE-ARE-THEY-NOW-Atlee-Hammaker-Ex-pitcher-2640128.php

cxxv Baseball reference.com, Ron Darling.

cxxv Ibid.

cxxvii Ibid.

cxxviii Ibid.

cxxix Eddy. March 2016.

cxxx Baseball reference.com, Ron Darling.

cxxxi NY Times Best Sellers List. April 2016.

cxxxii Hogue, Bob. February 18, 2015. Hawaii's Humble Hall Of Famer.

cxxxiii Baseball-reference.com. Mike Fetters.

cxxxiv Ibid.

cxxxv Pinto. 2011. Bleacher Report. 20 Greatest Pitching Stares of All Time.

cxxxvi Hogue, Bob. February 18, 2015. Hawaii's Humble Hall Of Famer.

cxxxvii Bloom. August 21, 2003.

cxxxviii Diamondbacks Press Release. November 17, 2016.

cxxxix Olney, Buster. "Escaping Hawaii and Finding Paradise,: New York Times, January 22, 2001.

cxl Curry, Jack. "Agbayani Living a Dream." New York Time, June 9, 1999.

cxli McCarron, Antony. "Hawaiian Punch: Mets' Agbayani Homers to Stardom." New York Daily News, June 20, 1999.

cxlii Baseballreference.com Benny Agbayani

cxliii Bertha, Mike. October 7, 2015. Today in Postseason History: Benny Agbayani hit a walk-off homer for the Mets in NLDS Game 3.

cxliv Baseballreference.com Benny Agbayani

cxlv Costello, Rory. Benny Agbayani

cxlvi McCarron, Anthony. April 10, 2010. Former New York Mets OF Benny Agbayani coming up big once again.

cxlvii Hawaii News.com. October 27, 2015 Benny Agbayani Talks World Series.

cxlviii Ocker, Sheldon (March 6, 2006). "Baseball takes Graves family back to Vietnam". Akron Beacon Journal.
cxlix University of Miami Sports Hall of Fame. Danny Graves.
cl BaseballReference.com Danny Graves
cli MLB.com. Danny Graves.

clii BaseballReference.com Danny Graves
cliii Sullivan, Michael. January 29, 2006. Bringing Baseball to Vietnam.

clivBlack Book Partners 2009. Johnny Damion Biography.
clv Baseball Reference.com Johnny Damon
clvi MLB.com. Johnny Damon

clvii Mahoney, Larry Former Red Sox Star Recall Career. Bangor Daily News. Jan. 15, 2015
clviii Mitchell, Houston (November 23, 2015) "Eight things you should know about Dave Roberts". L.A. Times.
clix Ibid.
clx Baseball-Reference.com Dave Roberts
clxi Browne, Ian. October 17, 2014. Roberts' Steal Set Amazing 2004 Playoff Run in Motion.
clxii Baseball-Reference.com Dave Roberts
clxiii Gurnick, Ken. Roberts is Dodgers' pick to be Manager. November 23, 2016.
clxiv Gurnick, Ken. Roberts is Dodgers' pick to be Manager. November 23, 2016. http://m.mlb.com/news/article/157933286/dave-roberts-named-dodgers-manager/

clxv Brown, Tim "Dave Roberts is evidence why race can be both important, meaningless". Yahoo Sports. December 1, 2015
clxvi Eskenazi. Stuart. November 20, 2008. Local Japanese Americans Applaud the Hiring of Don Wakamatsu.
clxvii Brewer, Jerry. "Don Wakamatsu's grandparents' story puts new spin on life, baseball". Seattle Times. April 5, 2009.
clxviii Baseball-Reference.com Don Wakamatsu

clxix Eskenazi, Stuart. November 20, 2008. Local Japanese Americans Applaud the Hiring of Don Wakamatsu.

clxx Divish, Ryan. April 30, 2016. Former Mariner Manager Don Wakamatsu Itching to Get Back into Leading Role.

clxxi Costello, Rory. Onan Masaoka. Society for American Baseball Research.

clxxii Baseball-Reference.com Onan Masaoka

clxxiii US Census Bureau . US 2010 Census Shows Asians Fastest Growing Race Group.

clxxiv Caple, Jim. April 22, 2011. The Ichiro-Matsui relationship.

clxxv Associated Press. "Suzuki Saluted with Major Award". July 1, 2004.

clxxvi Baseball-reference.com Kurt Suzuki

clxxvii Baseball-reference.com Kurt Suzuki

clxxviii Mlb.com. Kurt Suzuki.

clxxix Berardino, Mike. "Kurt Suzuki's New Secret Weapon: an ax handled bat" TwinCities.com June 20, 2016.

clxxx Okihiro, Michael. "Suzuki Is Living His Dream". The Hawaii Herald. October 6, 2014.

clxxxi Giants/mlb blog.

clxxxii Staples, Bill Jr. "Another hero in the family? The World War II history of Dix Ishikawa". Society for American Baseball Research, Spring 2016 Newsletter.

clxxxiii Baseball America. Travis Ishikawa.

clxxxiv Baseball-reference.com Travis Ishikawa

clxxxv Jenkins, Bruce. December 30, 2014 Ishikawa's NLCS Clinching Homer an Enduring Memory.

clxxxvi Baseball-reference.com Travis Ishikawa

clxxxvii Baseball-reference.com Travis Ishikawa

clxxxviii Baseball-reference.com Brandon League

clxxxix Rieper, Max. "Royals sign relievers Brandon League and Al Alburquerque to minor league deals". RoyalsReview.com January 7, 2017

cxc Vilonia, Bill. "Catholic grad Sadler comfortable in baseball transition". Pensacola New Journal. October 29, 2014

cxci Moeller, Jeff. Q&A with the Athletics' Shane Komine. MLBplayers.com Nov. 27, 2006

cxcii Baseball-reference.com Shane Komine

cxciii Dobrow, Marty. April 30, 2012.

cxciv Dobrow, Marty. April 20, 2012

cxcv Baseball-reference.com Charlie Zink

cxcvi Baseball-reference.com Charlie Zink

cxcvii Baseball-reference.com Duke Sardinha

cxcviii Baseball-reference.com Bronson Sardinha

cxcix Vrska, Kyle. "Sitting down with Bronson Sardinha". MiLB.com July 2, 2010

cc Parrillo, Ray (September 19, 2011). "Victorino earns MVP for charitable deeds". *Philly.com*. The Philadelphia Inquirer.

cci Baseball-reference.com Shane Victorino

ccii Adams, Steve. October 21, 2016.Shane Victorino on Future in Baseball.

cciii Baseball-reference.com Shane Victorino

cciv Hawaii News.com. Shane Victorino Goes Hollywood on Hawaii Five-0.

ccv MLB.com. Shane Victorino.

ccvi DiComo, Anthony. November 15, 2014. Guthrie Reconnects with Family, Heritage.

ccvii Guillermo, Emil "Guthrie-Ishikawa World Series Matchup Could Be Ethnic Milestone", nbcnews.com October 24, 2014

ccviii Fox Sports. April 17, 2015. Mission Man: Royals' Guthrie holds unique place in MLB history.

ccix Guillermo, Emil "Guthrie-Ishikawa World Series Matchup Could Be Ethnic Milestone", nbcnews.com October 24, 2014

[ccx] Baseball-reference.com Jeremy Guthrie

[ccxi] Baseball-reference.com Jeremy Guthrie

[ccxii] MLB.com Jeremy Guthrie

[ccxiii] Mackenzie, Joel. December 5, 2016. Aces to Secure World Series Starter.

[ccxiv] Reddington, Patrick. Nationals sign Jeremy Guthrie to Minor League deal with invite to Spring Training. Federalbaseball.com February 3, 2017

[ccxv] Espejo, Edwin. April 5, 2012 Clay Rapada: This Yankee is a Filipino

[ccxvi] Baseball-reference.com Clay Rapada

[ccxvii] Mlb.com. Clay Rapada.

[ccxviii] Ibid

[ccxix] MiLB.com. Greenjackets Announce 2017 Field Staff.

[ccxx] NEAATO Blog. https://neaat.wordpress.com/2008/08/05/first-filipino-in-big-leagues/

[ccxxi] Baseball-reference.com Geno Espineli

[ccxxii] Our Sports Central. July 3, 2008. 2008 PCL All Stars Announced.

[ccxxiii] Schulman, Henry. Espineli glad to forgo Olympics for the bigs. SFgate.com July 23, 2008.

[ccxxiv] Drellich, Evan. Espineli sees promise for baseball in Philippines. MiLB.com November 8, 2012.

[ccxxv] Medina, June. November 16, 2008. Fil-am Major League Pitcher Wins Top Baseball Award. https://web.archive.org/web/20111002125104/http://archives.manilatimes.net/national/2008/nov/16/yehey/sports/20081116spo3.html

[ccxxvi] Baseball-reference.com Tim Lincecum

[ccxxvii] Baseball-refererence.com Tim Lincecum

[ccxxviii] MLB.com Tim Lincecum

[ccxxix] MLB.com Tim Lincecum

[ccxxx] Baseball-reference.com Tim Lincecum

[ccxxxi] Boyle, Tim. February 2017. MLB: Tim Lincecum Not Ready to Retire, Move to the Bullpen.

ccxxxii Baseball-reference.com Chris Aguila

ccxxxiii Lara-Cinisomo, Vince. January 27, 2016. Sydney WBC Rosters Set.

ccxxxiv Baseball-reference.com Chris Aguila

ccxxxv "NBC News 4. January 7, 2016. MLB Players Start Nevada Baseball Factory.

ccxxxvi Baseball-reference.com Wes Littleton

ccxxxvii Costello, Rory. Benny Agbayani. Society for American Baseball Research.

ccxxxviii Baseball-reference.com Wes Littleton

ccxxxix Baseball-reference.com Matt Tuiasosopo

ccxl http://www.seattletimes.com/seattle-news/tuiasosopo-family-safe-throwin-samoan-calls-for-aid/; Costello, Rory. Benny Agbayani. Society for American Baseball Research

ccxli Baseball-reference.com Matt Tuiasosopo

ccxlii CBS Sports. October 31, 2016. Braves' Matt Tuiasosopo: Returns to Braves on minor league pact.

ccxliii Baseball-reference.com Brandon Villafuerte

ccxliv www.linkedin.com Brandon Villafuerte

ccxlv Baseball-reference.com Jason Bartlett

ccxlvi Butherus, J. Scott. Former Twins shortstop Jason Bartlett not your typical Naples retiree. Naples News. May 5, 2016.

ccxlvii Gonzales, Alden. May 10, 2013. Conger's Mother Marvels at Son's MLB Dream. http://m.angels.mlb.com/news/article/47074386/angels-catcher-hank-congers-mother-marvels-at-sons-mlb-dream/

ccxlviii Baseball-reference.com Hank Conger

ccxlix MLB.com. Hank Conger.

ccl BaseballAlmanac.com. Darryl Kile Award.

ccli Baseball-reference.com Hank Conger

cclii Adams, Steve. Diamondbacks, Hank Conger Agree to Minors Deal. MLBTradeRumors.com February 8, 2017 [ccliii] Waldstein, David. February 5, 2015. On Deck for the Yankees, From South Korea, Rob Refsnyder.

[ccliv] Waldstein, David. "On Deck for the Yankees, From South Korea, Rob Refsnyder". New York Times. February 5, 2015.

[cclv] Waldstein, David. "On Deck for the Yankees, From South Korea, Rob Refsnyder". New York Times. February 5, 2015.

[cclvi] MLB.com 2015 Prospect Watch.

[cclviicclvii] Baseball-reference.com Rob Refsnyder

[cclviii] Contursi, Steve. Yankees Rob Refsnyder: The Next Super-Utility Player. YanksGoYard.com January 11, 2017.

[cclix] Laurila, David. September 18, 2016. Sunday Notes: Refsnyder's Plan...

[cclx] Waldstein, David. "On Deck for the Yankees, From South Korea, Rob Refsnyder". New York Times. February 5, 2015.

[cclxi] Hartman, Kim. "Stereotypes don't trip up Wildcat slugger". Tuscon Sentinel. April 9, 2011.

[cclxii] Coffey, Wayne. He'll make you believe: Rob Refsnyder just may be the Yankees' solution at second base. New York Daily News. February 8, 2015.

[cclxiii] Baseball-reference.com Sean Manaea

[cclxiv] Mitrosilis, Teddy. March 14, 2013. MLB Spotlight on Sean Manaea.

[cclxv] Baseball-reference Sean Manaea

[cclxvi] Kaegel, Dick. "Royals draft two big lefties in Manaea, Reed". MLB.com June 6, 2013

[cclxvii] Halpine-Berger, Evan. Yankees Off-season Trade Target: Oakland Starter Manaea. YanksGoYard.com September 23, 2016.

[cclxviii] Hummel, Rick. July 6, 2015. Pham Making the Most of his Chance.

[cclxix] Goold, Derrick "cards prospect Reyes sweeps 'Tools Triple Crown' " St. Louis Post-Dispatch August 12, 2015.

[cclxx] Baseball-reference.com Tommy Pham

[cclxxi] Moeller, Jeff. May 5, 2011. Darwin Barney Earns Monthly Honors.

cclxxii Baseball-reference.com Darwin Barney

cclxxiii MLB.com Darwin Barney

cclxxiv Stull, Brian. April 15, 2014. Cards' Wong is a Hit in China. http://www.ksdk.com/sports/commentary/cards-wong-is-a-hit-in-china/282165592

cclxxv Frederickson, Ben. Kolten Wong's rise to majors has Hawaii buzzing with pride. FoxSports.com August 22, 2013.

cclxxvi Charpentier, Russ. Cape League: What's right for Wong? Cape Cod Times June 25, 2010.

cclxxvii Baseball-reference.com Kolten Wong

cclxxviii Ibid

cclxxix MLB.com Kolten Wong.

cclxxx ABS-CBN News. October 25, 2016. "Did you know? Chicago Cubs shortstop is half-Pinoy"

cclxxxi Baseball-reference.com Addison Russell

cclxxxii Mlb.com. Addison Russell

cclxxxiii Neveau, James. Addison Russell Hits Historic Garnd Slam in Game 6 NBCChicago.com November 1, 2016.

cclxxxiv Kim, Sung Min. Explaining South Korea's WBC Struggles. BaseballAmerica.com March 11, 2017

cclxxxv Brock, Corey. Ross' mom dedicated to kids on field and off. MLB.com May 9, 2013

cclxxxvi BaseballReference.com Tyson Ross

cclxxxvii Ball, Scott. "Tyson Ross - Family Man" PAC-12 News July 23, 2007 http://pac-12.com/article/2007/07/23/tyson-ross-family-man

cclxxxviii BaseballReference.com Joe Ross

cclxxxix Reddington, Patrick. Nationals Land Six Prospects on Keith Law's Top 100 Prospects List FederalBaseball.com January 29, 2015 http://www.federalbaseball.com/2015/1/29/7946865/nationals-land-six-prospects-on-keith-law-top-100-prospects-list ccxc Russell, Jake. Joe and Tyson Ross's mom sports split Nats-Padres jersey supporting both sons. WashngtonPost.com June 18, 2016

ccxci Lapchick, 2016 The 2016 Racial and Gender Report Card: Major   League   Baseball https://nebula.wsimg.com/811d6cc2d0b42f3ff087ac2cb690ebeb ?AccessKeyId=DAC3A56D8FB782449D2A&disposition=0&al loworigin=1

ccxcii Duncan, James. June 7, 2014. Top Ten Asian MLB Players of All-Time. time

ccxciii Lapchick, 2016, April.

ccxciv Lapchick, 2016, April.

ccxcv US Census. Population and Race.

ccxcvi US Census Facts and Features.

ccxcvii US Census Quick Facts.

ccxcviii MiLB.com. Minor League Baseball Diversity Initiative.

ccxcix   MiLB.com.   Field   Program. http://www.milb.com/milb/info/diversity_initiatives.jsp

ccc Footer, Alyson. December 9, 2016. Diversity, Inclusion Points of Emphasis at Winter Meetings. http://m.mlb.com/news/article/210795350/winter-meetings-at-center-of-mlbs-diversity/

ccci Lapchick, 2016, April.

cccii   MLB.com.   Urban   Youth   Academy. http://mlb.mlb.com/community/uya.jsp?id=about

ccciii Fordin, Spenser. August 5, 2015. Trio of UYA Players Get Division   I   Scholarships. http://m.mlb.com/news/article/141295576/urban-youth-academy-players-sign-with-colleges/

ccciv   MLB.com   Urban   Youth   Academy   Timeline. http://www.mlb.com/community/uya.jsp?id=timeline

cccv MLB Community. Reviving Baseball in the Inner Cities. http://web.mlbcommunity.org/programs/rbi.jsp?content=history

cccvi Fordin, Spenser. June 11, 2015. Draft shows impact of MLB diversity   initiatives http://m.mlb.com/news/article/130032766/draft-shows-impact-of-mlb-diversity-initiative

Index

Name	Page number
Agbayani, Benny	90
Aguila, Chris	132
Balcena, Bobby	46
Barney, Darwin	143
Bartlett, Jason	133
Conger, Hank	138
Damon, Johnny	97
Darling, Ron	83
Espineli, Geno	130
Fetters, Mike	86
Graves, Danny	93
Guthrie, Jeremy	123
Hammaker, Atlee	77
Honolulu Johnny, See Williams, John	35
Ishikawa, Travis	113
Kim, Wendell	65
Komine, Shane	115
Kurosaki, Ryan	73
League, Brandon	114
Lincecum, Tim	130
Littleton, Wes	132
Lum, Mike	58
Manaea, Sean	142
Masaoka, Onan	107
Murakami, Masanori	52
Oana, Henry	41
Pham, Tommy	142
Rapada, Clay	125
Refsnyder, Rob	139

Rego, Tony   40
Robello, Tony   41
Roberts, Dave   102
Ross, Joe   146
Ross, Tyson   146
Russell, Addison   145
Sadler, Billy   115
Sakata, Lenn   67
Sardinha, Bronson   117
Sardinha, Dane   117
Solaita, Tony   55
Suzuki, Kurt   111
Tuiasosopo, Matt   133
Victorino, Shane   121
Villafuerte, Brandon   133
Wakamatsu, Don   106
Wilcox, Milt   71
Williams, John   35
Wong, Kolten   144
Zenimura, Kenichi   26
Zink, Charlie   116

References

ABS-CBN News. October 25, 2016. "Did you know? Chicago Cubs shortstop is half-Pinoy" ABS-CBN News October 25, 2016. http://news.abs-cbn.com/sports/10/25/16/did-you-know-chicago-cubs-shortstop-is-half-pinoy

Adams, Steve. Diamondbacks, Hank Conger Agree to Minors Deal. MLBTradeRumors.com February 8, 2017.

Adams, Steve. October 21, 2016. Shane Victorino on Future in Baseball. http://www.mlbtraderumors.com/shane-victorino.

"American League Notes." Sporting Life, October 24, 1914. 16.

Ardolino, Frank. "Missionaries, Cartwright, and Spalding: The Development of Baseball in 19th Century Hawaii." Nine: A Journal of Baseball History and Culture. Volume 10 No. 2. Spring, 2002.

Associated Press, "51 Homers! Yanks Hope for Samoa the Same," *The Binghamton Press*, March 16, 1969.

Associated Press. "Suzuki Saluted with Major Award". July 1, 2004.

Ball, Scott. "Tyson Ross - Family Man" PAC-12 News July 23, 2007 http://pac-12.com/article/2007/07/23/tyson-ross-family-man

Barnes, Mike. March 1986. Atlee Hammaker Now Knows It Was a Mistake. http://www.upi.com/Archives/1986/03/19/Atlee-Hammaker-now-knows-it-was-a-mistakeHowever-the/2187511592400/. Accessed March 14, 2017.

Barton, Melissa. Immigration to Hawaii, www.ImmigrationtoUnitedStates.org Accessed June 30, 2016.

BaseballAlmanac.com. 1976 Cincinnati Reds Roster. http://www.baseball-almanac.com/teamstats/roster.php?y=1976&t=CN5.

BaseballAlmanac.com. Darryl Kile Award. http://www.baseball-almanac.com/awards/darryl_kile_award.shtml

Baseball America. Travis Ishikawa. http://www.baseballamerica.com/statistics/players/cards/19024. Accessed February 28, 2017.

Baseball Federation of Asia. Asian Baseball Championship. http://www.baseballasia.org/BFA/include/index.php?Page=8-1 Accessed March 17, 2016.

Baseball Federation of Asia: Hong Kong. http://www.baseballasia.org/BFA/include/index.php?Page=9-1-6

Baseball Federation of Asia. Thailand: History of Thai Baseball. Accessed March 17, 2016. http://www.baseballasia.org/BFA/include/index.php?Page=9-1-N Accessed March 17, 2016.

Baseballfever.com. http://www.baseball-fever.com/showthread.php?9017-Almost-Perfect-Perfect-Games. Accessed March 14, 2017.

Baseball-reference.com. 1960s. http://www.baseball-reference.com/bullpen/1960s

Baseball-reference.com. Addison Russell. http://www.baseball-reference.com/players/r/russead02.shtml. Accessed March 14, 2017.

Baseball-Reference.com. Atlee Hammaker. http://www.baseball-reference.com/players/h/hammaat01.shtml. Accessed November 10, 2016.

Baseballreference.com Benny Agbayani. http://www.baseball-reference.com/players/a/agbaybe01.shtml. Accessed November 10, 2016.

Baseball-reference.com. Bobby Balcena. http://www.baseball-reference.com/players/b/balcebo01.shtml. Accessed July 5, 2016.

Baseball-reference.com. Brandon League. http://www.baseball-reference.com/players/l/leagubr01.shtml. Accessed March 14, 2017.

Baseball-reference.com. Brandon Villafuerte. http://www.baseball-reference.com/players/v/villabr01.shtml. Accessed March 14, 2017.

Baseball-reference.com. Bronson Sardinha. Baseball-reference.com Bronson Sardinha. Accessed March 14, 2017.

Baseball-reference.com. Charlie Zink. http://www.baseball-reference.com/players/z/zinkch01.shtml. Accessed March 14, 2017.

Baseball-reference.com. Chris Aguila. http://www.baseball-reference.com/players/a/aguilch01.shtml. Accessed March 14, 2017.

Baseball-reference.com. Clay Rapada. http://www.baseball-reference.com/players/r/rapadcl01.shtml. Accessed March 14, 2017.

BaseballReference.com Danny Graves. http://www.baseball-reference.com/players/g/graveda01.shtml.

Baseball-reference.com. Darwin Barney. http://www.baseball-reference.com/players/b/barneda01.shtmlAccessed March 14, 2017.

Baseball-Reference.com. Dave Roberts. http://www.baseball-reference.com/players/r/roberda07.shtml Accessed October 30, 2016.

Baseball-Reference.com. Don Wakamatsu. http://www.baseball-reference.com/players/w/wakamdo01.shtml. Accessed October 30, 2016.

Baseball-reference.com. Duke Sardinha. http://www.baseball-reference.com/bullpen/Duke_Sardinha. Accessed March 14, 2017.

Baseball-reference.com. Geno Espineli. http://www.baseball-reference.com/players/e/espinge01.shtml. Accessed March 14, 2017.

Baseball-reference.com. Hank Conger. http://www.baseball-reference.com/players/c/congeha01.shtml Accessed March 14, 2017.

Baseball-reference.com. Jason Bartlett. http://www.baseball-reference.com/players/b/bartlja01.shtml Accessed March 14, 2017.

Baseball-reference.com. Jeremy Guthrie. http://www.baseball-reference.com/players/g/guthrje01.shtml. Accessed March 14, 2017.

BaseballReference.com. Joe Ross. http://www.baseball-reference.com/players/r/rossjo01.shtml Accessed March 14, 2017.

Baseball Reference.com Johnny Damon. http://www.baseball-reference.com/players/d/damonjo01.shtml. Accessed October 30, 2016.

Baseball-reference.com. "Johnny Williams Register Statistics and History." http://www.baseball-reference.com/players/w/willijo02.shtml Accessed June 29, 2016.

Baseball-reference.com Kolten Wong. http://www.baseball-reference.com/players/w/wongko01.shtml. Accessed March 14, 2017.

Baseball-reference.com. Kurt Suzuki. http://www.baseball-reference.com/players/s/suzukku01.shtml. Accessed October 30, 2016.

Baseball-reference.com. Lenn Sakata. http://www.baseball-reference.com/register/player.fcgi?id=sakata001len Accessed October 30, 2016.

Baseball-reference.com Masanori Murakami. http://www.baseball-reference.com/players/m/murakma01.shtml. Accessed August 3, 2016.

Baseball-reference.com. Matt Tuiasosopo. http://www.baseball-reference.com/players/t/tuiasma01.shtml. Accessed March 14, 2017.

Baseball-reference.com Mike Fetters. http://www.baseball-reference.com/players/f/fettemi01.shtml. Accessed March 14, 2017.

Baseball-reference.com Mike Lum. http://www.baseball-reference.com/players/l/lummi01.shtml. Accessed September 10, 2016.

Baseball-reference.com Milt Wilcox. http://www.baseball-reference.com/players/w/wilcomi01.shtml.

Baseball-Reference.com. Onan Masaoka. http://www.baseball-reference.com/players/m/masaoon01.shtml. Accessed September 10, 2016.

Baseball-reference.com "Prince Oana." http://www.baseball-reference.com/players/o/oanapr01.shtml Accessed July 3, 2016.

Baseball-reference.com. Rob Refsnyder. http://www.baseball-reference.com/players/r/refsnro01.shtml Accessed March 14, 2017.

Baseball reference.com, Ron Darling. http://www.baseball-reference.com/players/d/darliro01.shtml. Accessed March 14, 2017.

Baseball-reference.com Ryan Kurosaki. http://www.baseball-reference.com/players/k/kurosry01.shtml. Accessed March 14, 2017.

Baseball-reference.com. Sean Manaea. http://www.baseball-reference.com/players/m/manaese01.shtml Accessed March 14, 2017.

Baseball-reference.com. Shane Komine. http://www.baseball-reference.com/players/k/kominsh01.shtml. Accessed March 14, 2017.

Baseball-reference.com Shane Victorino. http://www.baseball-reference.com/players/v/victosh01.shtml. Accessed March 14, 2017.

Baseball-reference.com. Tim Lincecum. http://www.baseball-reference.com/players/l/linceti01.shtml. Accessed March 14, 2017.

Baseball-reference.com. Tommy Pham. http://www.baseball-reference.com/players/p/phamth01.shtml Accessed March 14, 2017.

Baseball-reference.com. "Tony Rego." http://www.baseball-reference.com/players/r/regoto01.shtml Accessed June 29, 2016.

Baseball-reference.com. "Tony Robello." http://www.baseball-reference.com/players/r/robelto01.shtml Accessed June 29, 2016.

Baseball-reference.com. Tony Solaita. http://www.baseballreference.com/players/s/solaito01.shtml. Accessed October 1, 2016.

Baseball-reference.com Travis Ishikawa. http://www.baseball-reference.com/players/i/ishiktr01.shtml. Accessed March 14, 2017.

BaseballReference.com. Tyson Ross. http://www.baseball-reference.com/players/r/rossty01.shtml Accessed March 14, 2017.

Baseball-reference.com Wendell Kim. http://www.baseball-reference.com/bullpen/Wendell_Kim. Accessed January 5, 2017.

Baseball-reference.com. Wes Littleton. http://www.baseball-reference.com/players/l/littlwe01.shtml Accessed January 5, 2017.

Bergman, Justin. "Will Chinese Baseball Make it to the Big Leagues?" 2011. Time Magazine.

Berardino, Mike. "Kurt Suzuki's New Secret Weapon: an ax handled bat" TwinCities.com June 20, 2016.

Bertha, Mike. October 7, 2015. Today in Postseason History: Benny Agbayani hit a walk-off homer for the Mets in NLDS Game 3. http://m.mlb.com/cutfour/2015/10/07/153569848/benny-agbayani-hits-walk-off-home-run-in-nlds

Black Book Partners 2009. Johnny Damion Biography. http://www.jockbio.com/Bios/Damon/Damon_bio.html.

Bloom. August 21, 2003.

Brewer, Jerry. "Don Wakamatsu's grandparents' story puts new spin on life, baseball". Seattle Times. April 5, 2009.

Brock, Corey. Ross' mom dedicated to kids on field and off. MLB.com May 9, 2013

Brown, Dave. February 16, 2015. Former Giants, Red Sox and Cubs coach Wendell Kim dies at 64. http://www.cbssports.com/mlb/news/former-giants-red-sox-and-cubs-coach-wendell-kim-dies-at-64/

Browne, Ian. October 17, 2014. Roberts' Steal Set Amazing 2004 Playoff Run in Motion.

http://m.mlb.com/news/article/98844328/dave-roberts-steal-set-amazing-2004-red-sox-playoff-run-in-motion/
Brown, Tim "Dave Roberts is evidence why race can be both important, meaningless". Yahoo Sports. December 1, 2015.

Bruske, Paul. "Detroit Duly Delighted." Sporting Life, January 31, 1914.

Boyle, Tim. February 2017. MLB: Tim Lincecum Not Ready to Retire, Move to the Bullpen.

Butherus, J. Scott. Former Twins shortstop Jason Bartlett not your typical Naples retiree. Naples News. May 5, 2016.

Call To The Pen. http://calltothepen.com/2017/01/22/mlb-tim-lincecum-not-ready-to-retire-move-to-the-bullpen/
Caple, Jim. April 22, 2011. The Ichiro-Matsui relationship. http://www.espn.com/mlb/columns/story?id=6408880&columnist=caple_jim.
CBS Sports. October 31, 2016. Braves' Matt Tuiasosopo: Returns to Braves on minor league pact. http://www.cbssports.com/mlb/players/playerpage/541519/matt-tuiasosopo.
Charpentier, Russ. Cape League: What's right for Wong? Cape Cod Times June 25, 2010.
Ciampaglia, Dante A. Jul 14, 2015. Masanori Murakami: Baseball's Forgotten Pioneer. Time.com/3955421/masanori-murakami/
Coffey, Wayne. He'll make you believe: Rob Refsnyder just may be the Yankees' solution at second base. New York Daily News. February 8, 2015.

Contursi, Steve. Yankees Rob Refsnyder: The Next Super-Utility Player. YanksGoYard.com January 11, 2017.

Costello, Rory. "Johnny Williams." Society for American Baseball Research. http://sabr.org/bioproj/person/7a544ac1 Accessed June 29, 2016.

Costello, Rory. Benny Agbayani. Society for American Baseball Research. http://sabr.org/bioproj/person/99c897f8. Accessed October 29, 2016.

Costello, Rory. Lenn Sakata. Society for American Baseball Research. http://sabr.org/bioproj/person/7cc84d2b Accessed October 29, 2016.

Costello, Rory. Onan Masaoka. Society for American Baseball Research. http://sabr.org/bioproj/person/63efd188. Accessed October 29, 2016.

Costello, Rory. "Prince Oana." Society for American Baseball Research. http://sabr.org/bioproj/person/7cc84d2b Accessed June 29, 2016.

Curry, Jack. "Agbayani Living a Dream." New York Time, June 9, 1999.

Dawes, Gavin. *History of the Hawaiian Islands.* Honolulu: University of Hawaii Press, 1968.

Diamondbacks Press Release. November 17, 2016. http://www.azsnakepit.com/2016/11/17/13669350/arizona-diamondbacks-2017-coaching-staff-announced.

DiComo, Anthony. November 15, 2014. Guthrie Reconnects with Family, Heritage. http://m.mlb.com/news/article/101532804/royals-pitcher-jeremy-guthrie-reconnects-with-family-heritage-in-japan/

Divish, Ryan. April 30, 2016. Former Mariner Manager Don Wakamatsu Itching to Get Back into Leading Role. http://www.seattletimes.com/sports/mariners/former-mariner-manager-don-wakamatsu-itching-to-get-back-into-leading-role/

Dobrow, Marty. April 30, 2012. Field of Brief Dreams. http://www.espn.com/boston/story/_/id/7831023/charlie-zink-made-fenway-park-one-game.

Drellich, Evan. Espineli sees promise for baseball in Philippines. MiLB.com November 8, 2012.

Duncan, James. June 7, 2014. Top Ten Asian MLB Players of All-Time. http://bleacherreport.com/articles/2088484-top-10-asian-mlb-players-of-all-

Durso, Joseph. "Solaita, Big Hitter from South Pacific, Bids for Starring Role in Yankee Cast," *The New York Times*, September 24, 1968.

Eddy, March 2016.

Ellsesser, Stephen. May 10, 2007. Zenimura A True Baseball Ambassador. http://m.mlb.com/news/article/1956563/206422570. Accessed March 14, 2017.

Eskenazi, Stuart. November 20, 2008. Local Japanese Americans Applaud the Hiring of Don Wakamatsu. http://www.seattletimes.com/sports/mariners/local-japanese-americans-applaud-the-mariners-hiring-of-don-wakamatsu/
Espejo, Edwin. April 5, 2012 Clay Rapada: This Yankee is a Filipino https://asiancorrespondent.com/2012/04/clay-rapada-this-yankee-is-a-filipino/#2PFeJl2VAJS2ux3h.99.

ETSU Hall of Fame Members. http://www.etsubucs.com/halloffame/members/. Accessed March 14, 2017.

Feldmann, Doug. (2009). The 1976 Cincinnati Reds: **Last Hurrah for the Big Red Machine**. McFarland.

Footer, Alyson. December 9, 2016. Diversity, Inclusion Points of Emphasis at Winter Meetings. http://m.mlb.com/news/article/210795350/winter-meetings-at-center-of-mlbs-diversity/

Fordin, Spenser. June 11, 2015. Draft shows impact of MLB diversity initiatives http://m.mlb.com/news/article/130032766/draft-shows-impact-of-mlb-diversity-initiative

Fordin, Spenser. August 5, 2015. Trio of UYA Players Get Division I Scholarships. http://m.mlb.com/news/article/141295576/urban-youth-academy-players-sign-with-colleges/

Fox Sports. April 17, 2015. Mission Man: Royals' Guthrie holds unique place in MLB history.

http://www.foxsports.com/mlb/story/kansas-city-royals-jeremy-guthrie-mormon-missionary-world-series-041715.

Franks, J.S. *Asian Pacific Americans in Baseball.* Jefferson, NC.: McFarland Books, 2008.

Frederickson, Ben. Kolten Wong's rise to majors has Hawaii buzzing with pride. FoxSports.com August 22, 2013.

Giants Blog. Giants/mlb blog. https://sfgiants.mlblogs.com/from-the-railroads-to-the-farms-to-the-baseball-fields-358cdf143096#.n6q1pssup

Goldberg, Hy. "Sports in the News," *The Newark News*, March 3, 1969

Gonzales, Alden. May 10, 2013. Conger's Mother Marvels at Son's MLB Dream. http://m.angels.mlb.com/news/article/47074386/angels-catcher-hank-congers-mother-marvels-at-sons-mlb-dream/

Goold, Derrick "cards prospect Reyes sweeps 'Tools Triple Crown' " St. Louis Post-Dispatch August 12, 2015.

Greene, Sam. Henry Oana file at National Baseball Hall of Fame Library, 1943. Originally published in the Detroit News.

Guillermo, Emil "Guthrie-Ishikawa World Series Matchup Could Be Ethnic Milestone", nbcnews.com October 24, 2014

Gurnick, Ken. Roberts is Dodgers' pick to be Manager. November 23, 2016. http://m.mlb.com/news/article/157933286/dave-roberts-named-dodgers-manager/

Halpine-Berger, Evan. Yankees Off-season Trade Target: Oakland Starter Manaea. YanksGoYard.com September 23, 2016.

Hartman, Kim. "Stereotypes don't trip up Wildcat slugger". Tuscon Sentinel. April 9, 2011.

Hawaii News.com. October 27, 2015 Benny Agbayani Talks World Series. http://www.hawaiinewsnow.com/story/30365646/benny-agbayani-talks-world-series.

Hawaii News.com. Shane Victorino Goes Hollywood on Hawaii Five-0. http://www.hawaiinewsnow.com/story/16971905/shane-victorino-goes-hollywood-on-hawaii-five-0. Accessed March 14, 2017.

Hayes, Anthony. "All American Pastime," May 25, 2000. www.asianweek.com

Hillinger, Charles. January 10, 1990. http://articles.latimes.com/1990-01-10/sports/sp-207_1_san-pedro

History.com First Japanese Player Makes MLB Debut. http://www.history.com/this-day-in-history/first-japanese-player-makes-mlb-debut

Hogue, Bob. February 18, 2015. Hawaii's Humble Hall Of Famer. http://www.midweek.com/hawaiis-humble-hall-famer/.

Horn, John. September 15, 2011. Milt Wilcox: From World Champion to Royal Oak Icon.

http://patch.com/michigan/royaloak/from-world-champion-to-royal-oak-icon.

Hummel, Rick. July 6, 2015. Pham Making the Most of his Chance. http://www.stltoday.com/sports/baseball/professional/article_70 c95f5b-a077-5249-bf91-f32fff6450a9.html

Jenkins, Bruce. December 30, 2014 Ishikawa's NLCS Clinching Homer an Enduring Memory. http://www.sfgate.com/giants/jenkins/article/Ishikawa-s-NLCS-clinching-homer-an-enduring-5984139.php#photo-7289350

Kaegel, Dick. "Royals draft two big lefties in Manaea, Reed". MLB.com June 6, 2013

Kaneshiro, Stacy. August 15, 2002. Kalani's Sakata, Kurosaki major achievers. http://the.honoluluadvertiser.com/article/2002/Aug/15/sp/sp07a.html.

Kaneshiro, Stacy. September 26, 2002. Passing up football was wise decision for Lum. http://the.honoluluadvertiser.com/article/2002/Sep/26/sp/sp06a.html

Keyser, Tom. "The Man Who Hit for Hammerin' Hank," *The Calgary Herald*, March 29, 1998, p. B7.

Kim, Sung Min. Explaining South Korea's WBC Struggles. BaseballAmerica.com March 11, 2017

Kim, Wendell, Rains, Sally Tippett. (1988) Youth Baseball: A Coach's and Parent's Guide (The Art & Science of Coaching Series). Coaches Choice.

Kritzer, Cy. "Happy Go Roars on Texas Trail." The Sporting News, July 31, 1946.

Kroner, Steve. April 17, 2005. WHERE ARE THEY NOW?: Atlee Hammaker / Ex-pitcher looks back with pride / Injuries that bedeviled his career with Giants left him frustrated.

http://www.sfgate.com/sports/article/WHERE-ARE-THEY-NOW-Atlee-Hammaker-Ex-pitcher-2640128.php. Accessed March 14, 2017.

Kruth, Cash. August 3, 2016. Baseball Softball to Return to the Olympics in 2020. http://m.mlb.com/news/article/193412904/baseball-will-return-to-2020-olympics-in-tokyo/ Accessed September 1, 2016.

Lapchick, 2016 The 2016 Racial and Gender Report Card: Major League Baseball https://nebula.wsimg.com/811d6cc2d0b42f3ff087ac2cb690ebeb?AccessKeyId=DAC3A56D8FB782449D2A&disposition=0&alloworigin=1

Lara-Cinisomo, Vince. January 27, 2016. Sydney WBC Rosters Set. http://www.baseballamerica.com/international/sydney-wbc-qualifier-schedule-set/#y3uh7MfG4BVbXVJl.97

Lara-Cinisomo, Vince. November 15, 2016. 2017 World Baseball Classic Schedule and Scores. http://www.baseballamerica.com/international/2017-world-baseball-classic-schedule/ Accessed March 14, 2017.

Lariosa, Joseph. June 26, 2013. Fil-Am was 1st Asian to play in major league baseball. http://www.filipinostarnews.net/sports/fil-am-was-1st-asian-to-play-in-major-league-baseball.html?189db0. Accessed August 5, 2016.

Laurila, David. September 18, 2016. Sunday Notes: Refsnyder's Plan... http://www.fangraphs.com/blogs/sunday-notes-refsnyders-plan-doziers-bananas-santana-hardy-wainwright-more/

Lemke, Bob. "Hawaii's Playboy Prince is a Collector's Challenge." Sports Collectors Digest, August 2, 1991.

LinkedIn. Brandon Villafuerte. https://www.linkedin.com/in/brandon-villafuerte-b7688956

Lum Performs Magic on Stage and at Bat," *The Sporting News*, September 26, 1981

Mackenzie, Joel. December 5, 2016. Aces to Secure World Series Starter. http://web.theabl.com.au/news/article.jsp?ymd=20161205&content_id=210360778&fext=.jsp&vkey=news_t4067&sid=t4067.

Macur, Juliet. "A Sport Banned by Mao Zedong Makes a Comeback." 2008. The New York Times. www.nytimes.com/2008/07/06/sports/06iht-base.1.14264507.html. Accessed March 8,2016.

Mahoney, Larry   Former Red Sox Star Recall Career. Bangor Daily News. Jan. 15, 2015

McCarron, Anthony. April 10, 2010. Former New York Mets OF Benny Agbayani coming up big once again. http://www.nydailynews.com/sports/baseball/mets/new-york-mets-benny-agbayani-coming-big-article-1.164472.

McCarron, Antony. "Hawaiian Punch: Mets' Agbayani Homers to Stardom." New York Daily News, June 20, 1999.

Medina, June. November 16, 2008. Fil-am Major League Pitcher Wins Top Baseball Award. https://web.archive.org/web/20111002125104/http://archives.manilatimes.net/national/2008/nov/16/yehey/sports/20081116spo3.html

MiLB.com. Greenjackets Announce 2017 Field Staff. http://www.milb.com/news/article.jsp?ymd=20170103&content_id=212727174&fext=.jsp&vkey=news_t478

MiLB.com. Minor League Baseball Diversity Initiative. http://www.milb.com/milb/info/diversity.jsp

MiLB.com. Field Program. http://www.milb.com/milb/info/diversity_initiatives.jsp

MiLB.com. Sakata returns to San Jose dugout. http://www.milb.com/news/article.jsp?ymd=20140108&content _id=66415994&fext=.jsp&vkey=pr_1110.

Minshew, Wayne. "Lum Best No. 4 Picket, Says Other Lum," *The Sporting News*, July 5, 1969.

Mitchell, Houston (November 23, 2015) "Eight things you should know about Dave Roberts". L.A. Times.

Mlb.com. Addison Russell. http://m.mlb.com/player/608365/addison-russell

Mlb.com. Clay Rapada. http://m.mlb.com/player/449060/clay-rapada.

MLB.com. Danny Graves. http://m.mlb.com/player/115056/danny-graves#.

MLB.com. Darwin Barney. http://m.mlb.com/player/446381/darwin-barney

MLB.com. Hank Conger. http://m.mlb.com/player/474233/hank-conger

MLB.com. Jeremy Guthrie. http://m.mlb.com/player/425386/jeremy-guthrie.

MLB.com. Johnny Damon. http://m.mlb.com/player/113028/johnny-damon.

MLB.com Kolten Wong http://m.mlb.com/player/543939/kolten-wong

Mlb.com. Kurt Suzuki. http://m.mlb.com/player/435559/kurt-suzuki.

MLB.com. Lenn Sakata. http://m.mlb.com/player/121627/lenn-sakata.

MLB.com. Milt Wilcox. http://m.mlb.com/player/124253/milt-wilcox.

MLB.com Mike Lum. http://m.mlb.com/player/117998/mike-lum.

MLB.com 2015 Prospect Watch. http://m.mlb.com/prospects/2015?list=nyy

MLB.com. Shane Victorino. http://m.mlb.com/player/425664/shane-victorino

MLB.com. Tim Lincecum. http://m.mlb.com/player/453311/tim-lincecum

MLB.com. Tony Solaita. http://m.mlb.com/player/122523/tony-solaita.

MLB.com. Urban Youth Academy. http://mlb.mlb.com/community/uya.jsp?id=about

MLB.com Urban Youth Academy Timeline. http://www.mlb.com/community/uya.jsp?id=timeline

MLB Community. Reviving Baseball in the Inner Cities. http://web.mlbcommunity.org/programs/rbi.jsp?content=history

Miller, Dick. "Samoa's Solaita No. 1 Angel," *The Sporting News*, September 11, 1976.

Mitrosilis, Teddy. March 14, 2013. MLB Spotlight on Sean Manaea. http://www.espn.com/college-sports/story/_/id/9050726/indiana-state-sean-manaea-steps-mlb-draft-spotlight-college-baseball

Moeller, Jeff. May 5, 2011. Darwin Barney Earns Monthly Honors. http://mlb.mlb.com/pa/news/article.jsp?ymd=20110505&content_id=18668526&vkey=mlbpa_news&fext=.jsp

Moeller, Jeff. Q&A with the Athletics' Shane Komine. MLBplayers.com Nov. 27, 2006.

Moratal, Christophe. "IOC Executive Board Supports Tokyo 2020 Package of New Sports for IOC Session. International Olympic Committee." https://www.olympic.org/news/ioc-executive-board-supports-tokyo-2020-package-of-new-sports-for-ioc-session. Accessed July 3, 2016.

Murray, Todd. August 29, 2015. Coach Lum loving life in Pirates' baseball system. http://www.dominionpost.com/Coach-Lum-loving-life-in-Pirates

Nakagawa, Kerry. Japanese-American Baseball in California: A History

National Baseball Hall of Fame. The First of Many: Masanori Murakami. Baseballhall.org/discover/the-first-of-many Accessed March 14, 2017.

NBC News 4. January 7, 2016. MLB Players Start Nevada Baseball Factory. http://mynews4.com/sports/content/mlb-players-start-nevada-baseball-factory-01-19-2016

NEAATO Blog. https://neaat.wordpress.com/2008/08/05/first-filipino-in-big-leagues/.

Nelson, Kevin and Greenwald, Hank. *The Golden Game: The Story of California Baseball.* Berkeley, CA: Heyday Books, 2004.

Neveau, James. Addison Russell Hits Historic Garnd Slam in Game 6 NBCChicago.com November 1, 2016.

NY Times Best Sellers List. April 2016.

Ocker, Sheldon (March 6, 2006). "Baseball takes Graves family back to Vietnam." Akron Beacon Journal.

Okihiro, Michael. "Suzuki Is Living His Dream". The Hawaii Herald. October 6, 2014.

Olney, Buster. "Escaping Hawaii and Finding Paradise,: New York Times, January 22, 2001.

Olympic Council of Asia. The Asian Games. http://www.ocasia.org/game/GamesL1.aspx?9QoyD9QEWPeJ2 ChZBk5tvA Accessed July 3, 2016.

Our Sports Central. July 3, 2008. 2008 PCL All Stars Announced. http://www.oursportscentral.com/services/releases/2008-pacific-coast-league-all-stars-announced/n-3673538.

Parrillo, Ray (September 19, 2011). "Victorino earns MVP for charitable deeds". *Philly.com*. The Philadelphia Inquirer.

Pinto. 2011. Bleacher Report. 20 Greatest Pitching Stares of All Time.

Prewitt, Alex. Ex-Detroit Tiger Milt Wilcox Has Gone to the Dogs. http://www.espn.com/espn/page2/index?id=5714622. Accessed March 14, 2017.

Rains, Sally Tippett. February 15, 2015. Whatever Happened to Wendell Kim? The Sad Story. http://www.stlsportspage.com/CARDSBASEBALL/tabid/91/en tryid/1908/whatever-happened-to-wendell-kim-the-sad-story.aspx

Reaves, Joseph A. *Taking in a Game: A History of Baseball in Asia*. Lincoln, NE: University of Nebraska Press, 2002.

Reddington, Patrick. Nationals Land Six Prospects on Keith Law's Top 100 Prospects List FederalBaseball.com January 29, 2015 http://www.federalbaseball.com/2015/1/29/7946865/nationals-land-six-prospects-on-keith-law-top-100-prospects-list

Reddington, Patrick. Nationals sign Jeremy Guthrie to Minor League deal with invite to Spring Training. Federalbaseball.com February 3, 2017.

Regalado, Samuel O. *Nikkei Baseball: Japanese American Players from Immigration and Internment to the Major Leagues*. Urbana IL: University of Illinois Press, 2013.

Rieper, Max. "Royals sign relievers Brandon League and Al Alburquerque to minor league deals". RoyalsReview.com January 7, 2017.

Russell, Jake. Joe and Tyson Ross's mom sports split Nats-Padres jersey supporting both sons. WashngtonPost.com June 18, 2016

Samoa News. "Tony Solaita Killed in Tafuna Shooting Saturday," *The Samoa News*, February 12, 1990.

Sandoval, Jim. "Tony Robello." Society for American Baseball Research. http://sabr.org/bioproj/person/e56da0e8 Accessed June 29, 2016.

Schulman, Henry. April 2014. For Atlee Hammaker, more ball in the family seemed like bad idea. http://www.sfgate.com/giants/article/For-Atlee-Hammaker-more-ball-in-the-family-5428192.php.

Schulman, Henry. July 23, 2008. Espineli glad to forgo Olympics for the bigs. SFgate.com.

Siegal, Morris. "This Hometown Boy Roots for Atlanta." The Washington Times, October 9, 1991.

Staples, Bill Jr. "Another hero in the family? The World War II

history of Dix Ishikawa". Society for American Baseball Research, Spring 2016 Newsletter.

Staples, Bill, Jr. "A Timeline of Asian-American Baseball." Society for American Baseball Research. www.sabr.org. Accessed June 29, 2016.

Stevenson, V.L. "Barry's Beauts Defeat Sailors." Honolulu Evening Bulletin, March 28, 1910. 7.

Stokes, Matthew. March 13, 2012. Relatives Influence, Inspire Hammaker, Woodall

http://www.berryvikings.com/GeneralNews/Articles/Relatives

Stull, Brian. April 15, 2014. Cards' Wong is a Hit in China. http://www.ksdk.com/sports/commentary/cards-wong-is-a-hit-in-china/282165592

Stump, Al. *Cobb*. Chapel Hill, NC: Algonquin Books, 1996.

Sullivan, Michael. January 29, 2006. Bringing Baseball to Vietnam. http://www.npr.org/templates/story/story.php?storyId=5177282

Sutton, Keith. With Two Out in the Ninth - The Almost No-Hitters. http://research.sabr.org/journals/with-two-out-in-the-ninth-the-almost-no-hitters. Accessed March 14, 2017.

University of Miami Sports Hall of Fame. Danny Graves. http://www.umsportshalloffame.com/danny-graves.html. Accessed March 14, 2017.

US Census Bureau. www.census.gov accessed 6.30.16.

US Census Bureau. Facts for Features. https://www.census.gov/newsroom/facts-for-features/2016/cb16-ff07.html

US Census Bureau. Population and Race. https://www.census.gov/topics/population/race.html

US Census Bureau. Quick Facts. https://www.census.gov/quickfacts/table/PST045216/00

US Census Bureau. US 2010 Census Shows Asians Fastest Growing Race Group. https://www.census.gov/newsroom/releases/archives/2010_census/cb12-cn22.html.

Vilonia, Bill. "Catholic grad Sadler comfortable in baseball transition". Pensacola New Journal. October 29, 2014.

Vrska, Kyle. "Sitting down with Bronson Sardinha". MiLB.com July 2, 2010

Waldstein, David. February 5, 2015. On Deck for the Yankees, From South Korea, Rob Refsnyder. https://www.nytimes.com/2015/02/06/sports/baseball/on-deck-for-the-yankees-from-south-korea-rob-refsnyder.html?_r=2

Watson, Don. "Breaking into Baseball." Honolulu Star Bulletin, October 14, 1932.

Whiting, Robert. *The Chrysanthemum and the Bat: The Game Japanese Play.* Tokyo: Permanent Press, 1977.

World Baseball Classic. http://www.worldbaseballclassic.com/. Accessed June 29, 2016.

World Baseball Softball Confederation. http://www.wbsc.org/news/mongolia-olympic-committee-to-boost-baseballsoftball-with-eyes-on-tokyo-2020-games/ Mongolia Olympic Committee to boost baseball/softball with eyes on Tokyo 2020 Games February 14, 2017.

World Series, Little League, accessed March 17, 2016. http://www.littleleague.org/World_Series.html

YMCA Archives. "Philip L. Gillett." Chicago, IL, 1901.